The Core Deconstructed

How to Deconstruct the Common Core State Standards So You Can Teach

ELA/Literacy for Elementary Practice Journal

Books by Sheron M. Brown

The Core Deconstructed: How to Deconstruct the Common Core State Standards So You Can Teach Series

for

ELA/Literacy for Kindergarten

ELA/Literacy for First Grade

ELA/Literacy for Second Grade

ELA/Literacy for Third Grade

ELA/Literacy for Fourth Grade

ELA/Literacy for Fifth Grade

ELA/Literacy for Sixth Grade

ELA/Literacy for Seventh Grade

ELA/Literacy for Eighth Grade

ELA/Literacy for Ninth & Tenth Grades

ELA/Literacy for Eleventh & Twelfth Grades

ELA/Literacy for Elementary Practice Journal

ELA/Literacy for Middle and High School Practice Journal

The Core Deconstructed

How to Deconstruct the Common Core State Standards So You Can Teach

ELA/Literacy for Elementary

Practice Journal

Sheron M. Brown

ESbD Publishing
Laurel, MD 20723-5613

Copyright © 2013 by Sheron M. Brown. All rights reserved.

No part of this publication except for the appendices may be reproduced, stored in a retrieval system, or transmitted in any form or by any means, electronic, mechanical, photocopying, recording, scanning, or otherwise, without the prior written permission of the author.

Limit of Liability/Disclaimer of Warranty: While the publisher and author have used their best efforts in preparing this book, they make no representations or warranties with respect to the accuracy or completeness of the contents of this book and specifically disclaim any implied warranties of merchantability or fitness for a particular purpose. No warranty may be created or extended by sales representatives or written sales materials. The advice and strategies contained herein may not be suitable for your situation. You should consult with a professional when appropriate. Neither the publisher nor the author shall be liable for any loss of profit or any other commercial damages, including but not limited to special, incidental, consequential, personal, or other damages.

The Core Deconstructed: How to Deconstruct the Common Core State Standards So You Can Teach - ELA/Literacy for Elementary Practice Journal

1. Education: Teaching Methods & Materials 2. Education: Language Arts

ISBN-10: 0988746689
ISBN-13: 978-0-9887466-8-8

Cover design by William Flowers of Mojo Graphic
Produced in the United States of America
ESbD Publishing
9701 Evening Bird Lane, Suite 1
Laurel, MD 20723-5613
240-755-8187
www.edsolutionsbydesign.com

Dedication

To Immanuel, Uriah and Princess.

Table of Contents

Introduction...*11*

Chapter 1: Grounding the Standards

Describing Success...*13*
From Novice to Expert...*16*
The Intersection...*17*
Who Needs to Know?...*19*

Chapter 2: Deconstructing the Standards

Domains of the Discipline...*20*
Are You Ready?...*23*
Phase 1: Dissect the Standard...*26*
Phase 2: Tiered Objective Stems - *Recall Level*...*28*
Phase 3: Tiered Objective Stems - *Refine Level*...*40*
Phase 4: Tiered Objective Stems - *Recode Level*...*41*
What About Standards with Multiple Indicators?...*58*
You Are Ready!...*81*

Chapter 3: Teaching the Standards

Writing Robust Objectives...*82*
Designing Robust Learning Experiences..*86*
Back to Grounding...*96*
Who Said So?...*97*

Notes to Remember...*98*

About the Author...*99*

References...*100*

Appendices
    Appendix A: Common Core State Standards for Reading Literature...*104*
    Appendix B: Common Core State Standards for Reading Informational Texts...*107*
    Appendix C: Common Core State Standards for Writing...*110*
    Appendix D: Common Core State Standards for Speaking and Listening...*115*
    Appendix E: Common Core State Standards for Language...*118*

Forward

My Core Deconstructed Project
Over the past few months I embraced the task of reflecting on the process of breaking down a Common Core standard for my 9th grade Language & Composition class. After reading Dr. Brown's book, *The Core Deconstructed*, I felt that I had all the tools I needed to begin.

How Did I Begin?
I chose the Common Core standard, RL 9-10.3 – *Analyze how complex characters develop over the course of a text, interact with other characters, and advance the plot or develop the theme* – as it reoccurred in a few units I taught. As this was such a "packed" standard, breaking it down was a bit challenging at first. However, I found that creating my own version of deconstruction matrix was the easiest way for me to visualize how this standard could be broken down into objectives to use throughout my unit.

My Process
I modeled my table after a few from Dr. Brown's book by placing levels of knowledge down the side and levels of learning across the top. From there, I found it very intuitive to scaffold objectives that I derived from the standard that built upon each other horizontally across the matrix. Once this was done, I took it a step further and numbered each box on the matrix with the idea that this would make targeted instruction for small groups easier to illustrate in my lesson plans (i.e.: HB and ME work on cell#6, MT and MG work on cell#9, etc.) This also made it very easy to track student progress towards mastery of this standard over the course of a unit. Additionally, I used the Objective Builder and Dr. Brown's sample objectives in her book to categorize appropriate thinking skills with Bloom's cognitive labels in order to make the process of deconstructing future standards quicker.

What Did I Discover?
Overall, I found that this system makes it easier for teachers to see the "big picture" and build towards the Practitioner/Expert level over the course of a few lessons rather than overwhelm students or unintentionally instill a sense of defeat in them if an objective were not met in by the end of a class. Since my deconstruction matrix is now a soft copy, over time I can link websites with enrichment or re-teaching exercises, online games, web-based assessments or supplemental texts to each cell in the matrix. This will enhance my ability to more effectively target instruction in my diverse classes. The beauty of this system is that each teacher can tailor the results of the process to their own teaching style and the needs of their individual students.

This **visual unit plan**, as I call it, makes it easy to determine which objectives can be taught in 1 class period versus those that should be ongoing. This helped with my weekly planning, as I was able to create packets for my students with scaffolded lessons and resources that clearly showed progress towards a final performance task. (In this case it was a critical analysis essay.) Students were able to see their need to master one objective before they could master the next objective (which all fell under the umbrella of one CCSS). For example, students had to first *"recognize themes that arise throughout a text,"* then *"organize relationship* *between themes and characters,"* before they could *"produce a thesis on the connection between themes and characters."* A novice teacher might not necessarily recognize the level to which such a packed standard must be broken down, but this *The Core Deconstructed* makes the process very intuitive.

Additionally, being able to pinpoint exactly where students are struggling in the process of mastering a standard is essential not only for a data-driven school, **but also for students**. Working in collaborative groups enabled those who mastered each step to help those who were still working toward mastery. It also led to **great reflective discussions in teacher-student conferences**, as students were able to see their progress and reflect on exactly where they were struggling.

My Most Significant Discovery
The biggest difference I have seen in my classrooms is in the area of metacognitive knowledge. Student writing as well as reflective thinking was much more detailed and students demonstrated more investment in their learning, as they were able to track themselves and see progress on very specific objectives along the way. In the past, I thought of objectives as more for the teacher than for the student, but this process has made me see the importance of each student understanding each objective within a unit. When students understood and tracked their progress towards mastering each objective, they wanted to improve! More so, they were able to see how all of their work from the unit was connected and scaffolded which made lessons much more engaging as they saw a purpose to each day.

The Clarity
The clarity I received from breaking down this single standard enabled me to see the scope of my unit and begged the question, *"What if I were to break down each standard of this unit, not just one?"* My plan is to create a deconstruction matrix that encompasses all standards and pull scaffolded objectives to teach throughout the year. You will want to do the same!

Heather Simson
Middle School ELA/Literacy Teacher
Washington, DC

Introduction

If you can't describe what you are doing as a process, you don't know what you are doing.
~W. Edward Deming

When the draft of the Common Core State Standards was released in 2009, I was intrigued by the idea of internationally benchmarked standards and proceeded to study them deeply. I wanted to understand how they were constructed, and better still, I wanted to prepare myself to support teachers in knowing how to teach them and leaders in knowing how to lead with them. I read the standards intensely, made connections to Best Practices in education and began to take them apart. I realized that the way we think about how to look at standards would have to change. (The language we hear is "instructional shifts.") I also realized that the only way for educators to genuinely comprehend the standards at their root, was for educators themselves to dissect the standards. I started a journey toward stripping the standards to get to their core.

On this journey, I began by enlisting texts by Marzano, Kaplan, Renzulli and others. I reached out to teachers, coaches, school leaders, and state leaders and later led the production of a Common Core based curriculum in 2010. As I watched it unfold in 2011, I observed teachers and leaders struggle to use a product created by external curriculum consultants and became affirmed that they had to do the work themselves. Not only did teachers need to have an understanding of the core of the standards, but those who led needed to as well. I witnessed school leaders' anxieties about not understanding the depth of the standards. They worried about if their observation comments were substantial enough. The leaders sensed the substantiveness that was lacking in their conversations with teachers as a result of not knowing the standards intimately.

I reflected on the 3-year experience for 12 months and emerged with the decision to help teachers and leaders deconstruct the standards–break them down into their constituent parts so that they could build them back up in the minds of students. This resulted in what I call *The Core Deconstructed.* It's a process for educators to dissect the standards for themselves so they know them intimately. It's also a process that allows for creativity in an era of accountability.

This work is not about one person or a group of people creating for teachers. It's about teachers, instructional leaders and curriculum leaders co-creating with each other and for themselves, so they can gain the deep insights and understanding *they want* in order to translate the standards into the type of learning that *their students need.*

This work also transcends established curriculum. If your system has a curriculum, deconstructing the standards works. If your system does not have a curriculum, deconstructing the standards works. The process works because it's not about resources, or graphic organizers, or textbooks, or pacing guides or any of the other components that make up a curriculum. Deconstructing the standard is about extracting the essential elements--basic to expert knowledge, critical thinking, conceptual understanding and the how of learning--to produce a tiered process for providing on-grade level instruction for all students no matter their current academic level. It's about seeing the multiple layers within a standard and making connections with other standards across bands, across grade levels and across areas--something I call standard mapping.

The practice journal is presented in a nontraditional format on purpose. The book is succinct with many visuals because I didn't want you to spend all of your time reading. Instead, I wanted you to spend your time doing--deconstructing. The book is filled with examples to help you visualize the process. The good thing about the process is once you've done it, it is done! I guarantee that once you effectively deconstruct the standards and plan your instruction according to the demands of the standards and the starting point of your students, you won't have to worry about any test because authentic instruction will ensure student success.

As you prepare to embark on this journey, please allow me to make a request of you. *My request: partner with me to hear the voices of educators–the frontline folks who have to do the hard work of effective delivery by leading and teaching with the standards.* After deconstructing your first standard share it with your colleagues and share it with me to share with other educators. You can share with me on Twitter at https://twitter.com/DrSBrown or email me directly at drsbrown@edsolutionsbydesign.com.

My goal is to see 1,000,000 empowered educators who know the standards intimately, collaborating across the country to yield the true success for students we all know is possible by 2015. This goal can only be accomplished with you.

Thanks for investing in our students. Now let our journey begin!

Chapter 1

Grounding the Standards

A successful man is one who can lay a firm foundation with the bricks others have thrown at him.
~David Brinkley

Describing Success.

The word common in some cases refers to being alike. When discussing the Common Core State Standards (CCSS), this definition can lead educators, parents and stakeholders to believe that the standards were designed as if all students were the same and to make all students the same. This places the emphasis on students being common; however, the emphasis should be on the standards. The *common* in CCSS speaks to the standards and denotes how success is defined for a particular situation, with the situation being preparedness for success in college and the world of work.

It's like the safety standards for your car. You'd like to know that at a minimum all car manufactures work with standards in mind for your safety, yet the standards don't preclude luxury car manufactures from creating cars that exceed the safety standards. The same is the case for education. The standards are minimum criteria and they do not preclude educators from cultivating learners whose performance exceed them. The standards simply represent a *general expectation* of what preparedness looks like for the world beyond 12th grade. Yet, before we can prepare students to exceed the general expectations, we must first understand the foundation and the multiple levels within the standards. We must get grounded.

The Smarter Balanced Assessment Consortium (SBAC), the Partnership for Assessment of Readiness for College and Careers (PARCC) and Benjamin Bloom have all provided the foundational information to help us ground ourselves in the standards. SBAC created Achievement Level Descriptors (ALD), PARCC created Performance Level Descriptors (PLD) and Bloom generated a framework for categorizing educational objectives. On the one hand, the descriptors are needed to understand the levels of success within a standard. On the other hand, Bloom's taxonomy helps to understand the levels of learning and performance within a standard. Looking at the two separately can possibly be confusing and yield frustration.

Looking at the descriptors and the taxonomy simultaneously can create a mental model for progressive success throughout a standard. Below are suggestions for aligning the ALDs and PLDs with the Bloom's cognitive processes (Anderson, et al., 2001). The suggestions are not absolutes, but they provide a way for you to combine your previous professional knowledge with this new information. You'll notice the descriptor definitions may fall under multiple cognitive processes. This is to represent how they can work together and how you, the professional, can think about what your students should be doing to advance in their learning and thinking.

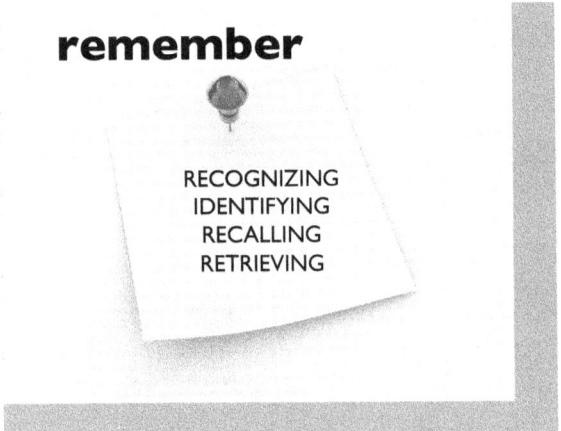

SBAC ALD 1: Student demonstrates **minimal** understanding of and ability to apply the knowledge and skills associated with college content-readiness.

SBAC ALD 2: Student demonstrates **partial** understanding of and ability to apply the knowledge and skills associated with college content-readiness.

PARCC PLD 1: A student who achieves a Level 1 demonstrates **minimal** command of the grade-level standards.

SBAC ALD 3: Student demonstrates **adequate** understanding of and ability to apply the knowledge and skills associated with college content-readiness.

PARCC PLD 2: A student who achieves a Level 2 demonstrates **partial** command of the grade-level standards.

PARCC PLD 3: A student who achieves a Level 3 demonstrates **moderate** command of the grade-level standards.

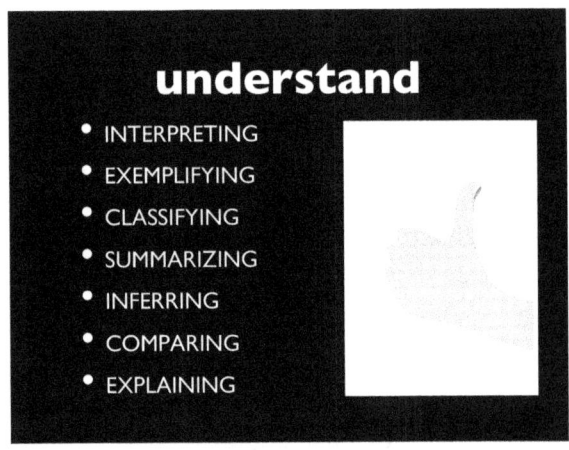

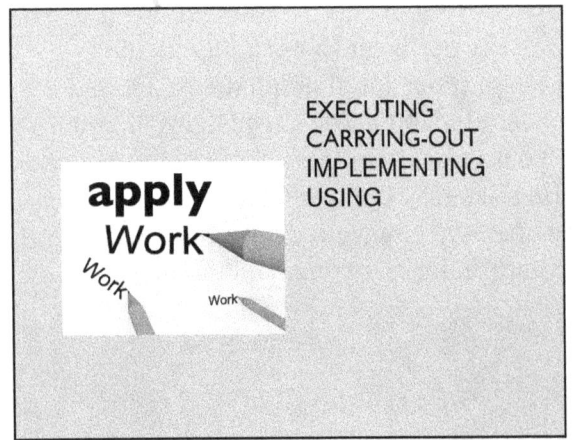

SBAC ALD 3: Student demonstrates **adequate** understanding of and ability to apply the knowledge and skills associated with college content-readiness.

PARCC PLD 2: A student who achieves a Level 2 demonstrates **partial** command of the grade-level standards.

PARCC PLD 3: A student who achieves a Level 3 demonstrates **moderate** command of the grade-level standards.

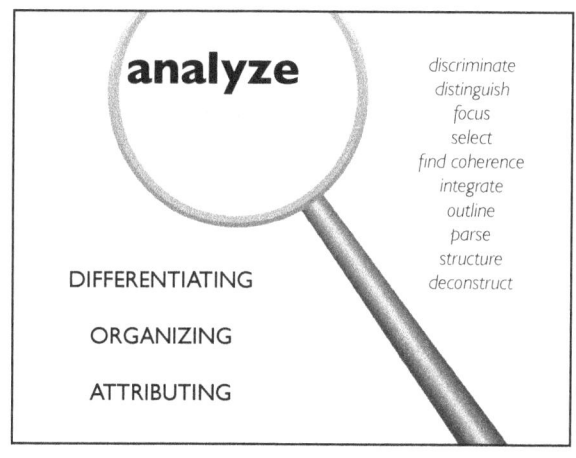

SBAC ALD 4: Student demonstrates **thorough** understanding of and ability to apply the knowledge and skills associated with college content-readiness.

PARCC PLD 4: A student who achieves a Level 4 demonstrates **strong** command of the grade-level standards.

SBAC ALD 4: Student demonstrates **thorough** understanding of and ability to apply the knowledge and skills associated with college content-readiness.

PARCC PLD 4: A student who achieves a Level 4 demonstrates **strong** command of the grade-level standards.

PARCC PLD 5: A student who achieves a Level 5 demonstrates **distinguished** command of the grade-level standards.

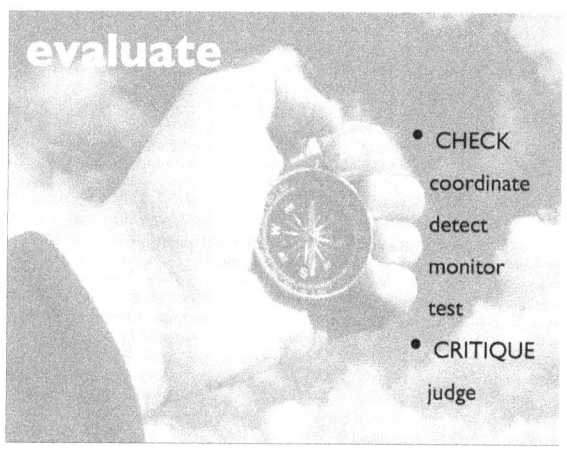

SBAC ALD 4: Student demonstrates **thorough** understanding of and ability to apply the knowledge and skills associated with college content-readiness.

PARCC PLD 5: A student who achieves a Level 5 demonstrates **distinguished** command of the grade-level standards.

From Novice to Expert.

Essentially, the standards require teachers to facilitate learning that transforms learners from novices to experts. Table 1 explains each category. In this era, educators must balance an understanding between the various terms: Bloom's cognitive processes, ALDs or PLDs and expert model. The list below *suggests* an alignment of the terms. Again these recommendations are not meant to be absolutes, but rather a means for professionals to balance all the terms relevant to the work of facilitating learning.

Transform Learners From Novice to Expert

Table I. Increasing Levels of Cognitive Demand and Learner Behaviors

Novice	Apprentice	Practitioner	Expert
• Learners experience content concretely • Learners manage micro-concepts one at a time • Learners require guided practice and skill • Learners need reinforcement, reassurance, and guidance • Learners seek out confirmation that validates their competency to complete a task	• Learners understand how micro-concepts connect within a discipline • Learners connect information within a micro-concept • Learners begin describing generalizations and themes that connect concepts • Learners apply skills with limited supervision • Learners seek out confirmation at task completion • Learners reflect on content and skills when prompted	• Learners simultaneously manage multiple micro-concepts • Learners construct generalizations to explain connections between concepts • Learners choose and use appropriate skills for task completion • Learners seek out feedback when needed • Learners demonstrate commitment and perseverance with reasonable challenges • Learners reflect on content and skills to refine understanding and performance	• Learners use concepts within and among disciplines in order to infer theories and principles • Learners generate innovations within the field and/or practice • Learners rehearse skill development independently and in order to advance self-improvement • Learners seek out the input of other experts for a specific purpose • Learners experience the flow state and gain pleasure during task completion that requires advanced skill or knowledge • Learners are independent and self-directed • Learners seek out experiences that cause them to once again advance through the levels

Adapted from Hedrick, K and Flannagan, J. S. (2009).

Novice	**Apprentice:**	**Practitioner:**	**Expert:**
Bloom: Remember	Bloom: Understand & Apply	Bloom: Analyze & Evaluate	Bloom: Create
SBAC: ALD 1 & 2	SBAC: ALD3	SBAC: ALD 4	SBAC: ALD 4
PARCC: PLD 1	PARCC: PLD 2 & 3	PARCC: PLD 4 & 5	PARCC: PLD 5

The Intersection.

You know the cognitive process dimensions of Bloom's Taxonomy: remember, understand, apply, analyze, evaluate and create. But are you as aware of the knowledge dimensions?

The *knowledge dimensions* represent the four types of knowledge that individuals employ when engaging in the cognitive processes. The chart below explains each type.

Type	Subtype	Description	Example
Factual Knowledge	• Terminology • Specific details • Elements	The basic elements students must know to be acquainted with a discipline or solve problems it	*A compound sentence is comprised of two clauses, a comma, and a conjunction.*
Conceptual Knowledge	• Classifications • Categories • Principles • Generalizations • Theories, models and structures	The interrelationships among the basic elements within a larger structure that enable them to function together	*A comma, a member of the punctuation family, serves to create a natural pause between two clauses.*
Procedural Knowledge	• Subject-specific skills • Algorithms • Subject-specific techniques and methods • Criteria for determining when to use appropriate procedures	How to do something, methods and inquiry, and criteria for using skills, algorithms, techniques, and methods	*When writing a compound sentence, place the comma after the first clause, followed by the conjunction and a second clause.*
Metacognitive Knowledge	• Strategic knowledge • Knowledge of cognitive tasks • Self-Knowledge	Knowledge of cognition in general as well as awareness and knowledge of one's own cognition	*I often make comma splices, so I have to remember to add a conjunction after the comma in a compound sentence.*

Adapted from Anderson, et al. (2001). *A taxonomy for learning teaching and assessing: A revision of Bloom's taxonomy of educational objectives.*

What happens when the two dimensions intersect along with the novice to expert model?

The Core Deconstructed

Standard: The actual standard goes here.

	Novice-Apprentice **Remember/Understand**	Apprentice-Practitioner **Apply/Analyze**	Practitioner-Expert **Evaluate/Create**
Factual Knowledge	The standard deconstructed for the cognitive processes of remember and understand in the factual knowledge dimension.	The standard deconstructed for the cognitive processes of apply and analyze in the factual knowledge dimension.	The standard deconstructed for the cognitive processes of evaluate and create in the factual knowledge dimension.
Conceptual Knowledge	The standard deconstructed for the cognitive processes of remember and understand in the conceptual knowledge dimension.	The standard deconstructed for the cognitive processes of apply and analyze in the conceptual knowledge dimension.	The standard deconstructed for the cognitive processes of evaluate and create in the conceptual knowledge dimension.
Procedural Knowledge	The standard deconstructed for the cognitive processes of remember and understand in the procedural knowledge dimension.	The standard deconstructed for the cognitive processes of apply and analyze in the procedural knowledge dimension.	The standard deconstructed for the cognitive processes of evaluate and create in the procedural knowledge dimension.
Metacognitive Knowledge	The standard deconstructed for the cognitive processes of remember and understand in the metacognitive knowledge dimension.	The standard deconstructed for the cognitive processes of apply and analyze in the metacognitive knowledge dimension.	The standard deconstructed for the cognitive processes of evaluate and create in the metacognitive knowledge dimension.

The Core Deconstructed (TCD) shows you how to break down the standards for each grade level so that you know *immediately* what should be taught. Students will experience deep learning daily by moving from novice to expert at every grade level, on every standard.

Who Needs to Know?

Leaders and Teachers

Table II. The Benefits of Knowing How to Deconstruct the Core

Instructional Leaders and Coaches	Curriculum Leaders	Teachers
• Instructional leaders and coaches can use the four phases of deconstruction to coach teachers through the process of understanding the depth of instruction required. This will help students to truly master a standard.	• Curriculum leaders can use four phases of deconstruction to write objective stems for teachers. Teachers can later use the objective stems to plan comprehensive day-by-day units that allow students to truly master a standard. The objective stems can also guide teachers on how to differentiate for the varying levels of abilities represented in their classrooms.	• Teachers can use the four phases of deconstruction, along with a tool called The Objective Builder, to write complete objectives that guide a comprehensive lesson design and built-in performance tasks. Hence aligned assessments are ensured.

What Can You Do with TCD?

TCD improves effectiveness, supports differentiation and increases rigor. Use the TCD to:

- Create your pre-unit assessments
- Modify instruction
- Design tiered lessons for struggling learners and advanced learners
- Write performance tasks
- Meet the needs of your special education population
- Teach each standard deeply to move all students from novice to expert
- Generate ideas quickly for learning stations

Deliberate teaching choices made daily will lead to deep learning.

Chapter 2

Deconstructing the Standard

The only place where success comes before work is in the dictionary.
~Donald Kendall

Domains of the Discipline.

Let me be upfront: deconstructing the standards is going to take work. The first time may not be an easy task, but the second time is easier than the first. The third time is easier than the second. The fourth time is easier than the third and so on. With each standard that you deconstruct, you become more skilled at the process, you begin to see more clearly the connections between all standards and at the end you know them intimately. This alone improves students' success. Furthermore, once they are done, they are done! Here's what Heather had to say about her experience:

> *"Overall, I found that this system makes it easier for teachers to see the 'big picture' and build towards the Practitioner/Expert level over the course of a few lessons rather than overwhelm students or unintentionally instill a sense of defeat in them if an objective is not met in by the end of a class. Since my TCD matrix is a soft copy, over time I could see linking websites with enrichment or re-teaching exercises, online games and quizzes or supplemental texts to each box on the grid in order to more effectively target instruction in my classes. The beauty of this system is that each teacher can tailor it to their own teaching style and the needs of their individual students."*

Essentially, a deconstructed standard is one that has been broken down or dismantled into its constituent parts. In this case, the constituent parts are where the cognitive processes and knowledge dimensions intersect. In order to break down the standard, you have to consider two things: (1) the level of thinking and (2) the aspect of the discipline being taught. We've already reviewed the levels of thinking--cognitive processes--in chapter 1. That leaves the aspects of the discipline, or the Discipline Domains. So what are they?

There are three major domains of each discipline that are referred to as depth, complexity and content imperatives (DCI) (Kaplan, Guzman & Tomlinson, 2009). Each domain has several domain types that are outlined on the following page. If you have never deliberately considered the discrete aspects of the discipline you teach, then a brief description is in order to support your understanding.

Domain of Discipline Depth

This domain addresses the amount of knowledge, intelligence, wisdom and insight evident in a product of mind. In this case, the product of mind is the discipline itself. The areas that represent knowledge products of the discipline are the language of the discipline, big ideas, patterns, rules, trends, unanswered questions, essential questions and ethics.

Domain of Discipline Complexity

This domain addresses the many interrelated parts or facets of the discipline. The three types of facets that make up the complexity domain are change over time, multiple perspectives and connections across disciplines.

Domain of Discipline Imperatives

The domain of imperatives represents the information that is absolutely necessary for the discipline to exist. To be clear, this information is a requirement and unavoidable otherwise there would be no discipline. The four discipline imperatives are the origin, the major contributions made, the convergence of ideas, the parallels within the discipline and the paradoxes.

The chart on the page that follows outlines the domains, the domain types and key phrases that serve as abbreviated descriptions. An understanding of the domains allows teachers to think and teach in a manner that allows students to deliberately engage in disciplinary thinking. Comprehending the domains leads to a robust deconstruction process that helps teachers to support students in performing at the highest level of the standards.

Discipline Domains

Domain of Discipline Depth		Domain of Discipline Complexity		Domain of Discipline Imperatives	
Depth Types	**Descriptions**	**Depth Types**	**Descriptions**	**Depth Types**	**Descriptions**
Language of the Discipline	Terms, nomenclature used by the disciplinarian or expert (or used within the discipline)	**Change Over Time**	Past, present, future; across during various time periods; change	**Origin**	The beginning, root, or source of an idea or event
Big Idea (generalization, principle, theory, concept)	Broad conclusions based on evidence, rules based on tested and accepted facts or assumptions; basic truths; laws or assumptions			**Contributions**	The significant part or result of an idea or event
Patterns	Designs, models, recurring elements, cycles, order, composite of characteristics			**Convergence**	The coming together or meeting point of events or ideas
Rules	Standards, organizational patterns, structure, order	**Multiple Perspectives**	Differing points of view, opinions based on varied roles and responsibilities; attitudes when considering or viewing	**Parallel**	Ideas or events that are similar and can be compared to one another
Trends	General tendency of direction, drift; influences over time causing effects to happen				
Unanswered Questions	Knowledge yet to be discovered, explored, proven; unclear information needing further evidence or support				
Essential Details	Features, attributes, elements, specific information, elaboration, embellishment	**Across Disciplines**	Connections, relationships within, between and among various disciplines or subject areas	**Paradox**	The contradictory elements in an event or idea
Ethics	Value-laden ideas, information; ideas, opinions related to bias, prejudice, discrimination				

Adapted from Kaplan, S., Guzman, I., and Tomlinson, C. (2009).

Are You Ready?

Now that you understand the two considerations, it's time to get to the actual work of deconstructing a standard.

Four phases make up the process.

Phase 1: Dissect the standard

Phase 2: Generate tiered objective stems for remember/understand

Phase 3: Generate tiered objective stems for apply/analyze

Phase 4: Generate tiered objective stems for evaluate/create

The steps in each phase are detailed for you to follow. Additionally, examples of deconstructed standards--one for each of the major college and career readiness areas for your grade level--are shared.

Practice as you move through the pages that follow. Once you've repeated the phases a few times, the process becomes more fluid and you begin to gain a richer understanding of each standard.

Before moving on to deconstructing, take this opportunity to engage in a short reflection and note your initial understanding so far. Consider what questions you may have at this point to prepare for the process.

TCD Journal Response

_____

_____
_____
_____
_____
_____
_____
_____
_____
_____

The end. Here's a sample standard after it's been deconstructed.

	THE CORE DECONSTRUCTED		
	RL.K.6 With prompting and support, name the author and illustrator of a story, and define the role of each in telling the story.		
	REMEMBER/ UNDERSTAND	**APPLY/ANALYZE**	**EVALUATE/CREATE**
Factual Knowledge Dimension	Students can **explain** the meaning of specific terminology: *author, illustrator, story, define, role (and other Tier 2 or 3 words related to the content or text)*	Students can **use** specific terminology: *author, illustrator, story, define, role (and other Tier 2 or 3 words related to the content or text)*	Students can **check** their use of specific terminology: *author, illustrator, story, define, role (and other Tier 2 or 3 words related to the content or text)*
Conceptual Knowledge Dimension	Students can **recognize** a *story* by its features Students can **identify** the *author and illustrator* of a *story* Students can **explain** the *roles* of *authors* and *illustrators*	Students can **find coherence** between the *author's* and the *illustrator's roles*	Students can **generate** a conclusion about *author's and illustrator's role in telling a story*
Procedural Knowledge Dimension	Students know how to **define** with specific information	Students know how to **attribute** specific information to *author's* and *illustrator's* roles	Students know how to **monitor** *author's* and *illustrator's roles* by their contributions to the story
Metacognitive Knowledge Dimension	Students are able to **recall** the details of the terms and concepts and how to receive support	Students are able to **ask** for directions that are relevant to complete a task	Students are able to **monitor** patterns in their behavior when support is needed
	Novice/Apprentice	**Apprentice/Practitioner**	**Practitioner/Expert**

The beginning. Now let's begin the process of deconstructing a standard.

A Quick Note Before Phase 1

As you will see shortly, the first phase of deconstructing a standard includes developing a conceptual understanding statement. A conceptual understanding statement is made up of concepts. Erickson (2007) explains that concepts are mental constructs or *organizing ideas* that allow for a deeper level of understanding and allows students to transfer their learning. Concepts can also be thought of as abstract ideas, generalized ideas or classes of things. To be clear, a brief list of concepts is listed below.

Change	System	Diversity	Point of View
Friendship	Nationalism	Relationships	Emotions
Immigration	Character	Courage	Influence
Violence	Self-Esteem	Leadership	Oppression
Idea	Wisdom	Time	War

Conceptual understanding statements are simple to create. They are comprised of two or more ideas or concepts that are incorporated within a sentence that represents a complete idea that is relevant for life or a discipline (Erickson). These statements are important because they serve as anchors for learning. They can be thought of as the reason for learning. As a note, some may refer to conceptual understanding statements as principles, generalizations or enduring understandings.

Thankfully, well-written standards have embedded concepts. Part of the deconstruction process is extracting the concepts in order to draft conceptual understanding statements. Writing these statements are simple. Consider the representation below to see how simple it is to write one.

Conceptual Understanding = 2 or more concepts brought together in 1 life generalization.

Consider the concepts change, friendship and time. Here are 2 examples of life generalizations:

Over time friendships change.
or
Time allows for our friendships to become stronger or diminished.

Depending on the theme or the book of focus, a teacher would be able to use the conceptual understanding as an anchor for the unit and as a motivator for authentic learning. In the spaces below practice writing a conceptual understanding statement, then move on to deconstructing!

_____
_____
_____
_____
_____

Phase 1: Dissect the Standard

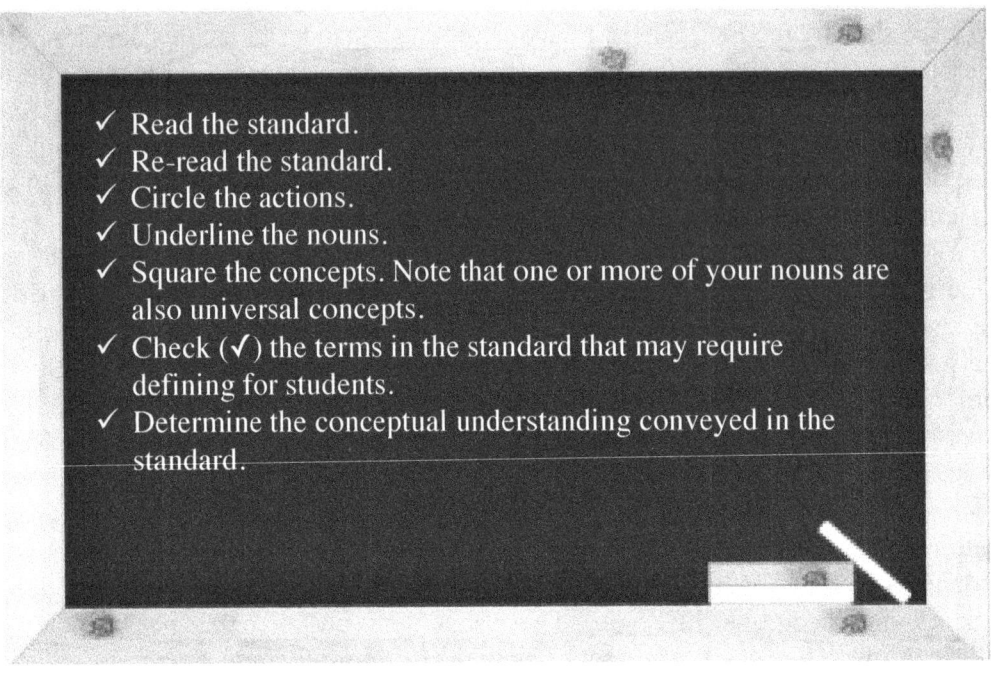

- ✓ Read the standard.
- ✓ Re-read the standard.
- ✓ Circle the actions.
- ✓ Underline the nouns.
- ✓ Square the concepts. Note that one or more of your nouns are also universal concepts.
- ✓ Check (✓) the terms in the standard that may require defining for students.
- ✓ Determine the conceptual understanding conveyed in the standard.

Example Standard RL.K.6.: With prompting and support, name the author and illustrator of a story and define the role of each in telling the story.

Conceptual Understanding:
Authors and illustrators have different roles in telling a story.

Example Standard RL.1.6.: Identify who is telling the story at various points in a text.

Conceptual Understanding:
Different characters can add to a story at different points in the story.

Example Standard RL.2.6.: Acknowledge differences in the points of view of characters, including by speaking in a different voice for each character when reading dialogue aloud.

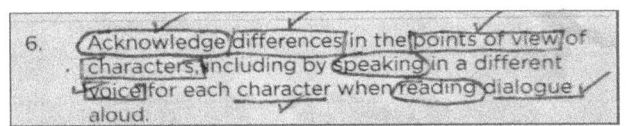

Conceptual Understanding:
A character's point of view can be heard through their "voice."

Example Standard RL.3.6.: Distinguish their own point of view from that of the narrator or those of the characters.

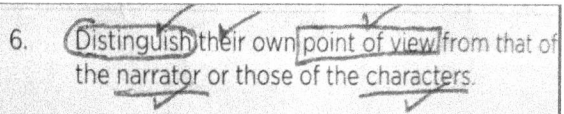

Conceptual Understanding:
My point of view could make the telling of a story different from the narrator or characters.

Example Standard RL.4.6.: Compare and contrast the point of view from which different stories are narrated, including the difference between first- and third-person narrations.

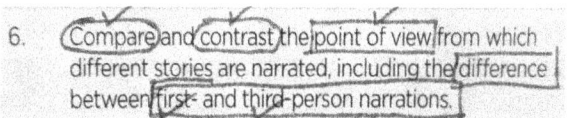

Conceptual Understanding:
Third person narrators may have a limited point of view in comparison to first-person narrators.

Example Standard RL.5.6.: Describe how a narrator's or speaker's point of view influences how events are described.

Conceptual Understanding:
An individual's point of view (or perspective) influences the way they present narratives.

Given the identified concepts in your grade level standard, what other conceptual understanding statement could have been written?

_____

_____

_____

_____

Phase 2: Tiered Objective Stems - Recall Level

Generate your "Remember/Understand" objective stems for *factual knowledge*. This includes terms and specific details.

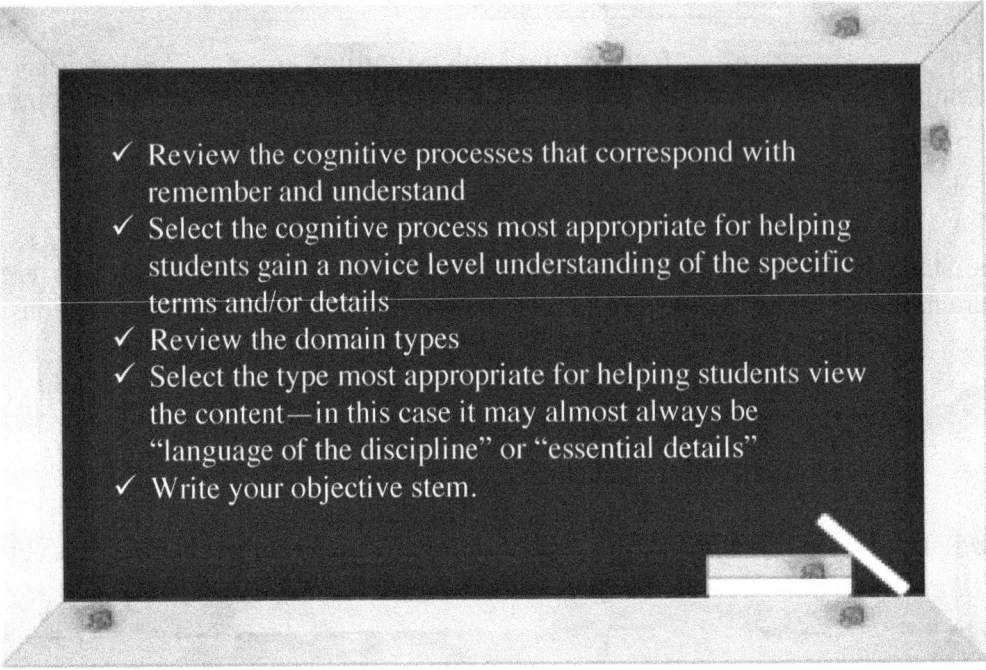

Example Standard RL.K.6.: With prompting and support, name the author and illustrator of a story and define the role of each in telling the story.

Factual knowledge tiered objective stem(s):
✓ Students can **explain** the meaning of specific *terminology*: author, illustrator, story, define, role

Explanation of objective stem(s):
✓ Explain aligns with the cognitive process of understand.
✓ Terminology represents the discipline domain of depth--specifically, language of the discipline.

Example Standard RL.1.6.: Identify who is telling the story at various points in a text.

Factual knowledge tiered objective stem(s):
- ✓ Students can **explain** the meaning of specific *terminology*: identify, story, various, points, text

Explanation of objective stem(s):
- ✓ Explain aligns with the cognitive process of understand.
- ✓ Terminology represents the discipline domain of depth--specifically, language of the discipline.

Example Standard RL.2.6.: Acknowledge differences in the points of view of characters, including by speaking in a different voice for each character when reading dialogue aloud.

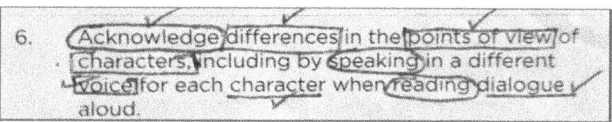

Factual knowledge tiered objective stem(s):
- ✓ Students can **explain** the meaning of specific *terminology*: acknowledge, difference, point of view, character, voice, dialogue

Explanation of objective stem(s):
- ✓ Explain aligns with the cognitive process of understand.
- ✓ Terminology represents the discipline domain of depth--specifically, language of the discipline.

Example Standard RL.3.6.: Distinguish their own point of view from that of the narrator or those of the characters.

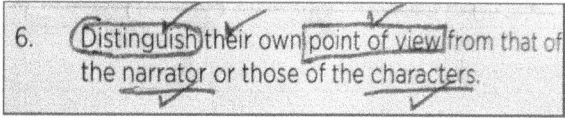

Factual knowledge tiered objective stem(s):
- ✓ Students can **exemplify** the meaning of specific *terminology*: distinguish, point of view, narrator, character

Explanation of objective stem(s):
- ✓ Exemplify aligns with the cognitive process of understand.
- ✓ Terminology represents the discipline domain of depth--specifically, language of the discipline.

Example Standard RL.4.6.: Compare and contrast the point of view from which different stories are narrated, including the difference between first- and third-person narrations.

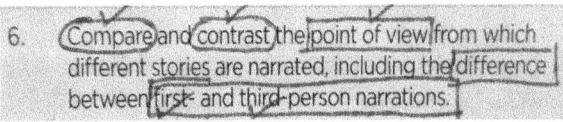

Factual knowledge tiered objective stem(s):
  ✓ Students can **exemplify** the meaning of specific *terminology*: compare, contrast, point of view, first-, third-person narration

Explanation of objective stem(s):
  ✓ Exemplify aligns with the cognitive process of understand.
  ✓ Terminology represents the discipline domain of depth--specifically, language of the discipline.

Example Standard RL.5.6.: Describe how a narrator's or speaker's point of view influences how events are described.

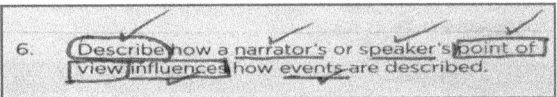

Factual knowledge tiered objective stem(s):
  ✓ Students can **paraphrase** the meaning of specific *terminology*: narrator, speaker, point of view, influence, event, describe

Explanation of objective stem(s):
  ✓ Paraphrase aligns with the cognitive process of understand.
  ✓ Terminology represents the discipline domain of depth--specifically, language of the discipline.

TCD Reflection: Note your understanding, insights or questions so far.

_____
_____
_____
_____
_____
_____
_____

Phase 2: Tiered Objective Stems - Recall Level

Generate your "Remember/Understand" objective stems for *conceptual knowledge*. This includes classifications, generalizations and models.

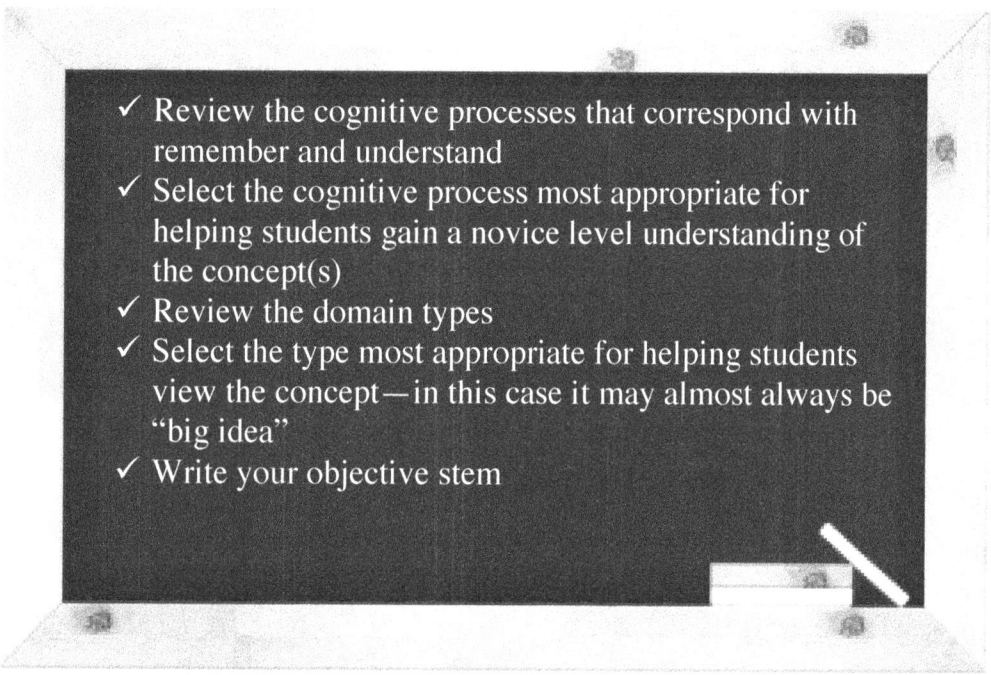

Example Standard RL.K.6.: With prompting and support, name the author and illustrator of a story and define the role of each in telling the story.

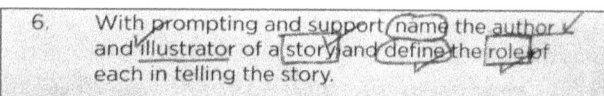

Conceptual knowledge tiered objective stem(s):
✓ Students can **recognize** a story by its *features*
✓ Students can **identify** the author and illustrator of a *story*
✓ Students can **explain** the *roles* of authors and illustrators

Explanation of objective stem(s):
✓ Recognize, identify and explain align with the cognitive process of understand.
✓ Features, story and roles represent the discipline domain of depth, imperatives and complexity--specifically, essential details, contributions and multiple perspectives, respectively.

Example Standard RL.1.6.: Identify who is telling the story at various points in a text.

Conceptual knowledge tiered objective stem(s):
- ✓ Students can **explain** the *features* of a story
- ✓ Students can **identify** the *various points* in a story
- ✓ Students can **identify** the speaker *various points* in a story

Explanation of objective stem(s):
- ✓ Explain, and identify align with the cognitive process of understand.
- ✓ Features and various points represent the discipline domain of depth and complexity--specifically, essential details and multiple changes over time, respectively.

Example Standard RL.2.6.: Acknowledge differences in the points of view of characters, including by speaking in a different voice for each character when reading dialogue aloud.

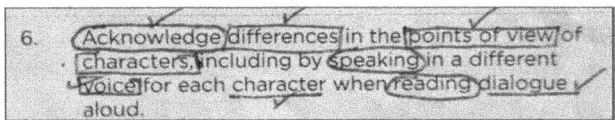

Conceptual knowledge tiered objective stem(s):
- ✓ Students can **identify** the *differences* in point of view between characters
- ✓ Students can **identify** the *differences* in "voice" between characters

Explanation of objective stem(s):
- ✓ Identify aligns with the cognitive process of understand.
- ✓ Differences represents the discipline domain of depth and complexity--specifically, multiple perspectives.

Example Standard RL.3.6.: Distinguish their own point of view from that of the narrator or those of the characters.

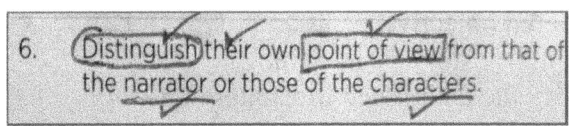

Conceptual knowledge tiered objective stem(s):
- ✓ Students can **contrast** the *details* between my point of view and the narrator's or character's

Explanation of objective stem(s):
- ✓ Contrast aligns with the cognitive process of understand.
- ✓ Details represents the discipline domain of depth--specifically, essential details.

Example Standard RL.4.6.: Compare and contrast the point of view from which different stories are narrated, including the difference between first- and third-person narrations.

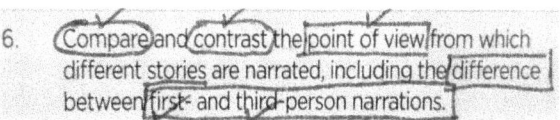

Conceptual knowledge tiered objective stem(s):
   ✓ Students can **classify** the *attributes* of first and third person
Explanation of objective stem(s):
   ✓ Classify aligns with the cognitive process of understand.
   ✓ Attributes represents the discipline domain of depth and complexity--specifically, essential details.

Example Standard RL.5.6.: Describe how a narrator's or speaker's point of view influences how events are described.

Conceptual knowledge tiered objective stem(s):
   ✓ Students can **explain** how assumptions *influence point of view*
Explanation of objective stem(s):
   ✓ Explain aligns with the cognitive process of understand.
   ✓ Influence and point of view represents the discipline domain of depth and complexity--specifically, trends and multiple perspectives, respectively.

TCD Reflection: Note your understanding, insights or questions so far.

_____

_____

_____

_____

_____

_____

_____

_____

Phase 2: Tiered Objective Stems - Recall Level

Generate your "Remember/Understand" objective stems for *procedural knowledge*. This includes skills, techniques, methods and procedures.

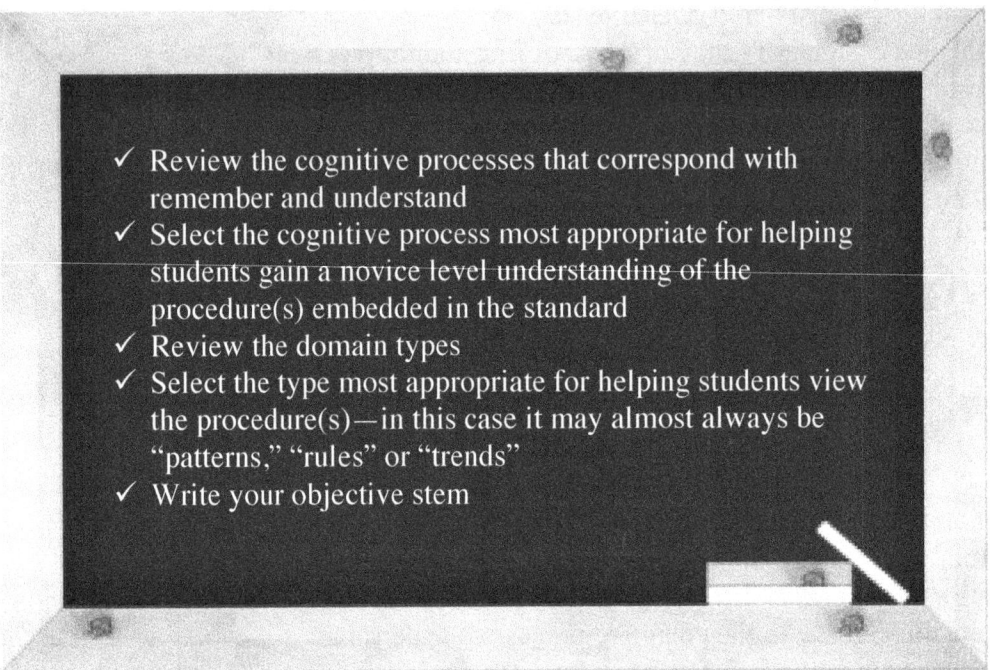

Example Standard RL.K.6.: With prompting and support, name the author and illustrator of a story and define the role of each in telling the story.

Procedural knowledge tiered objective stem(s):
    ✓ Students know how to **define** with specific *information*
Explanation of objective stem(s):
    ✓ Define aligns with the cognitive process of understand.
    ✓ Information represents the discipline domain of depth--specifically, essential details.

Example Standard RL.1.6.: Identify who is telling the story at various points in a text.

Procedural knowledge tiered objective stem(s):
- ✓ Students know how to **explain** the *process* used to identify

Explanation of objective stem(s):
- ✓ Explain aligns with the cognitive process of understand.
- ✓ Process represents the discipline domain of depth--specifically, rules.

Example Standard RL.2.6.: Acknowledge differences in the points of view of characters, including by speaking in a different voice for each character when reading dialogue aloud.

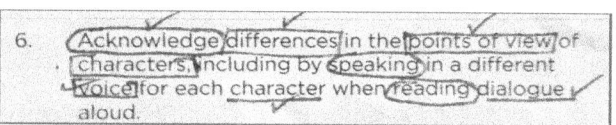

Procedural knowledge tiered objective stem(s):
- ✓ Students know how to **explain** the *process* used to acknowledge
- ✓ Students know how to **infer** voice *patterns* of different characters when reading aloud

Explanation of objective stem(s):
- ✓ Explain and infer align with the cognitive process of understand.
- ✓ Process and patterns represents the discipline domain of depth--specifically, rules and patterns, respectively.

Example Standard RL.3.6.: Distinguish their own point of view from that of the narrator or those of the characters.

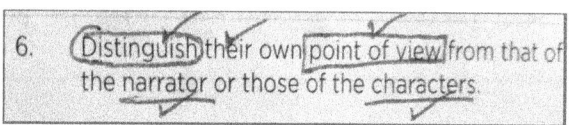

Procedural knowledge tiered objective stem(s):
- ✓ Students know how to **explain** the *steps* used to distinguish

Explanation of objective stem(s):
- ✓ Explain aligns with the cognitive process of understand.
- ✓ Steps represent the discipline domain of depth--specifically, rules.

Example Standard RL.4.6.: Compare and contrast the point of view from which different stories are narrated, including the difference between first- and third-person narrations.

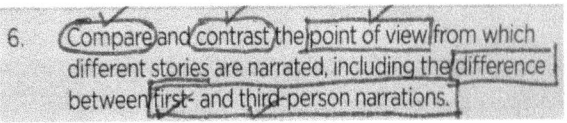

Procedural knowledge tiered objective stem(s):
- ✓ Students know how to **explain** the *steps* used to compare
- ✓ Students know how to **explain** the *steps* used to contrast

Explanation of objective stem(s):
- ✓ Explain aligns with the cognitive process of understand.
- ✓ Steps represents the discipline domain of depth--specifically, rules.

Example Standard RL.5.6.: Describe how a narrator's or speaker's point of view influences how events are described.

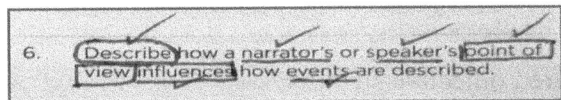

Procedural knowledge tiered objective stem(s):
- ✓ Students know how to **construct** a *model* that shows the structure of a description

Explanation of objective stem(s):
- ✓ Construct aligns with the cognitive process of understand.
- ✓ Model represents the discipline domain of depth--specifically, patterns.

TCD Reflection: Note your understanding, insights or questions so far.

_____
_____
_____
_____
_____
_____
_____

Phase 2: Tiered Objective Stems - Recall Level

Generate your "Remember/Understand" objective stems for *metacognitive knowledge*. This includes awareness of helpful tactics, awareness of task requirements and awareness of one's ability and support needed for task success.

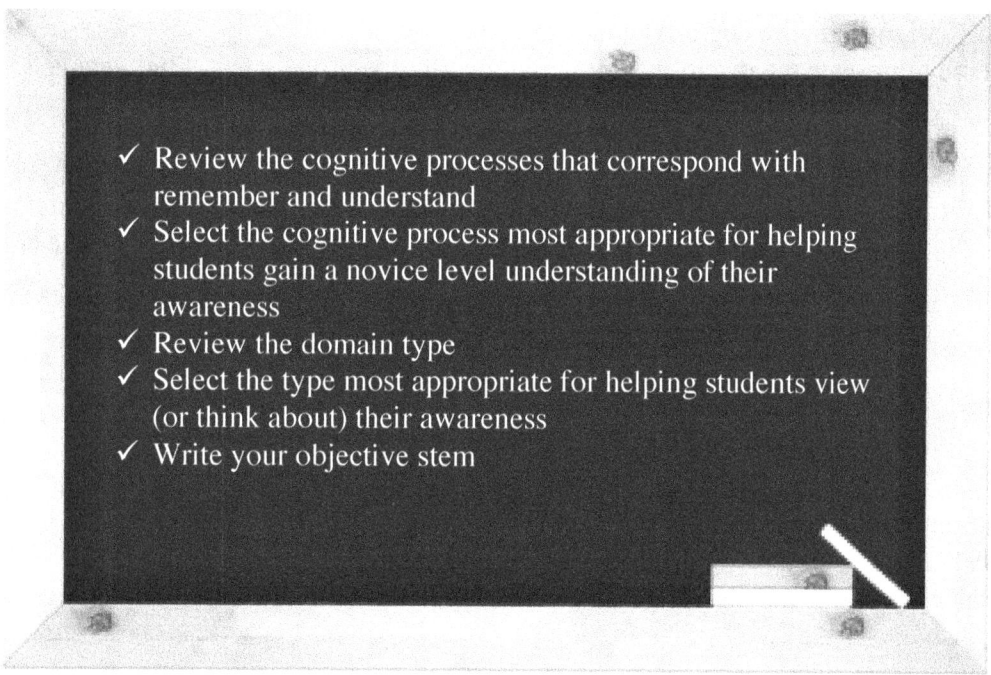

Example Standard RL.K.6.: With prompting and support, name the author and illustrator of a story and define the role of each in telling the story.

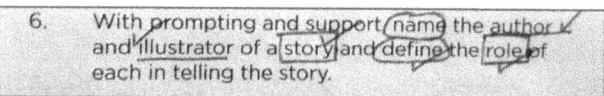

Metacognitive knowledge tiered objective stem(s):
- ✓ Students are able to **recall** the *details* of the terms and concepts and how to receive support

Explanation of objective stem(s):
- ✓ Recall aligns with the cognitive process of understand.
- ✓ Details represents the discipline domain of depth--specifically, essential details.

Example Standard RL.1.6.: Identify who is telling the story at various points in a text.

Metacognitive knowledge tiered objective stem(s):
  ✓ Students are able to **recall** the *details* of the terms and concepts
Explanation of objective stem(s):
  ✓ Recall aligns with the cognitive process of understand.
  ✓ Details represents the discipline domain of depth--specifically, essential details.

Example Standard RL.2.6.: Acknowledge differences in the points of view of characters, including by speaking in a different voice for each character when reading dialogue aloud.

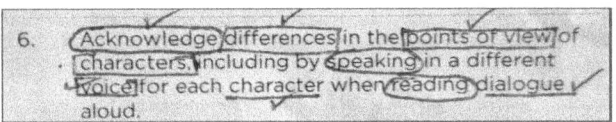

Metacognitive knowledge tiered objective stem(s):
  ✓ Students are able to **recall** the *details* of the terms and concepts
Explanation of objective stem(s):
  ✓ Recall aligns with the cognitive process of understand.
  ✓ Details represents the discipline domain of depth--specifically, essential details.

Example Standard RL.3.6.: Distinguish their own point of view from that of the narrator or those of the characters.

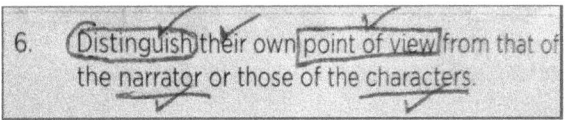

Metacognitive knowledge tiered objective stem(s):
  ✓ Students are able to **recall** the *details* of the terms and concepts
Explanation of objective stem(s):
  ✓ Recall aligns with the cognitive process of understand.
  ✓ Details represents the discipline domain of depth--specifically, essential details.

Example Standard RL.4.6.: Compare and contrast the point of view from which different stories are narrated, including the difference between first- and third-person narrations.

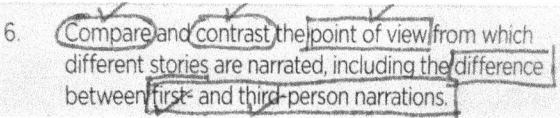

Metacognitive knowledge tiered objective stem(s):
- ✓ Students are able to **recall** the *details* of the terms and concepts

Explanation of objective stem(s):
- ✓ Recall aligns with the cognitive process of understand.
- ✓ Details represents the discipline domain of depth--specifically, essential details.

Example Standard RL.5.6.: Describe how a narrator's or speaker's point of view influences how events are described.

Metacognitive knowledge tiered objective stem(s):
- ✓ Students are able to **represent** the *details* required for completing the task

Explanation of objective stem(s):
- ✓ Represent aligns with the cognitive process of understand.
- ✓ Details represents the discipline domain of depth--specifically, essential details.

TCD Reflection: Note your understanding, insights or questions so far.

_____
_____
_____
_____
_____
_____
_____

Phases 3 and 4 follow the same pattern. Phase 3 is the process for creating Apply/Analyze tiered objective stems and Phase 4 is the process for Evaluate/Create. See the steps below.

Phase 3: Tiered Objective Stems - Refine Level

Generate Apply/Analyze Objective Stems for:

Factual Knowledge (terms, specific details)
- ✓ Review the cognitive processes that correspond with apply and analyze.
- ✓ Select the cognitive process most appropriate for helping students integrate their understanding of the specific terms and/or details on an apprentice/practitioner level.
- ✓ Review and select the domain type most appropriate for helping students view the content.
- ✓ Write your objective stem.

Conceptual Knowledge (classifications, generalizations, models)
- ✓ Review the cognitive processes that correspond with apply and analyze.
- ✓ Select the cognitive process most appropriate for helping students integrate their understanding of the concept(s) on an apprentice/practitioner level.
- ✓ Review and select the domain type most appropriate for helping students view the concept.
- ✓ Write your objective stem.

Procedural Knowledge (skills, techniques, methods, procedures)
- ✓ Review the cognitive processes that correspond with apply and analyze.
- ✓ Select the cognitive process most appropriate for helping students integrate their understanding of the procedure(s) on an apprentice/practitioner level.
- ✓ Review and select the domain type most appropriate for helping students view the procedure(s).
- ✓ Write your objective stem.

Metacognitive Knowledge (awareness of helpful tactics, task requirements, one's ability and support needed for task success)
- ✓ Review the cognitive processes that correspond with apply and analyze.
- ✓ Select the cognitive process most appropriate for helping students integrate their understanding of their awareness on an apprentice/practitioner level.
- ✓ Review and select the domain type most appropriate for helping students view (or think about) their awareness.
- ✓ Write your objective stem.

Your notes about Phase 3:

_____

_____

_____

_____

Phase 4: Tiered Objective Stems - Recode Level

Generate Evaluate/Create Objective Stems for:

Factual Knowledge (terms, specific details)
- ✓ Review the cognitive processes that correspond with evaluate and create.
- ✓ Select the cognitive process most appropriate for helping students meaningfully use their integrated understanding of the specific terms and/or details on an apprentice/practitioner level.
- ✓ Review and select the domain type most appropriate for helping students view the content.
- ✓ Write your objective stem.

Conceptual Knowledge (classifications, generalizations, models)
- ✓ Review the cognitive processes that correspond with evaluate and create.
- ✓ Select the cognitive process most appropriate for helping students meaningfully use their integrated understanding of the concept(s) on an apprentice/practitioner level.
- ✓ Review and select the domain type most appropriate for helping students view the concept.
- ✓ Write your objective stem.

Procedural Knowledge (skills, techniques, methods, procedures)
- ✓ Review the cognitive processes that correspond with evaluate and create.
- ✓ Select the cognitive process most appropriate for helping students meaningfully use their integrated understanding of the procedure(s) on an apprentice/practitioner level.
- ✓ Review and select the domain type most appropriate for helping students view the procedure(s).
- ✓ Write your objective stem.

Metacognitive Knowledge (awareness of helpful tactics, task requirements, one's ability and support needed for task success)
- ✓ Review the cognitive processes that correspond with evaluate and create.
- ✓ Select the cognitive process most appropriate for helping students meaningfully use their integrated understanding of their awareness on an apprentice/practitioner level.
- ✓ Review and select the domain type most appropriate for helping students view (or think about) their awareness.
- ✓ Write your objective stem.

Your notes about Phase 4:

_____

_____

_____

_____

Now is an ideal time to repeat the phases and **practice** going through the sample already presented. You may find that your tiered objective stems are **slightly different** from the ones here and that's fine. The most **important** point is that you consider all aspects of the standard to fully understand what it requires of teachers and students.

A few more standards follow after practice and reflection. **Practice** deconstructing those also. *After engaging in the process a few times, you will begin to notice how **fluent** you become at **deconstructing** the core.*

	THE CORE DECONSTRUCTED		
	RL.K.6 With prompting and support, name the author and illustrator of a story, and define the role of each in telling the story.		
	REMEMBER/ UNDERSTAND	**APPLY/ANALYZE**	**EVALUATE/CREATE**
Factual Knowledge Dimension	Students can **explain** the meaning of specific terminology: *author, illustrator, story, define, role (and other Tier 2 or 3 words related to the content or text)*	Students can **use** specific terminology: *author, illustrator, story, define, role (and other Tier 2 or 3 words related to the content or text)*	Students can **check** their use of specific terminology: *author, illustrator, story, define, role (and other Tier 2 or 3 words related to the content or text)*
Conceptual Knowledge Dimension	Students can **recognize** a *story* by its features Students can **identify** the *author and illustrator* of a *story* Students can **explain** the *roles* of *authors* and *illustrators*	Students can **find coherence** between the *author's* and the *illustrator's roles*	Students can **generate** a conclusion about *author's and illustrator's role in telling a story*
Procedural Knowledge Dimension	Students know how to **define** with specific information	Students know how to **attribute** specific information to *author's* and *illustrator's* roles	Students know how to **monitor** *author's* and *illustrator's roles* by their contributions to the story
Metacognitive Knowledge Dimension	Students are able to **recall** the details of the terms and concepts and how to receive support	Students are able to **ask** for directions that are relevant to complete a task	Students are able to **monitor** patterns in their behavior when support is needed
	Novice/Apprentice	**Apprentice/Practitioner**	**Practitioner/Expert**

	THE CORE DECONSTRUCTED		
	RL.1.6 Identify who is telling the story at various points in a text.		
	REMEMBER/ UNDERSTAND	**APPLY/ANALYZE**	**EVALUATE/CREATE**
Factual Knowledge Dimension	Students can **explain** the meaning of specific terminology: *identify, story, various, points, text (and other Tier 2 or 3 words related to the content or text)*	Students can **use** specific terminology: *identify, story, various, points, text (and other Tier 2 or 3 words related to the content or text)*	Students can **check** their use of specific terminology: *identify, story, various, points, text (and other Tier 2 or 3 words related to the content or text)*
Conceptual Knowledge Dimension	Students can **explain** the features of a *story* Students can **identify** the *various points* in a *story* Students can **identify** the speaker *various points* in a *story*	Students can **differentiate** between speakers in a *story* at *various points*	Students can **generate** a conclusion about *who tells a story at various points*
Procedural Knowledge Dimension	Students know how to **explain** the process used to *identify*	Students know how to **use** the process of *identifying*	Students know how to **monitor** their process of *identifying*
Metacognitive Knowledge Dimension	Students are able to **recall** the details of the terms and concepts	Students are able to **select** relevant information to complete a task	Students are able to **judge** the details in their work for self-correction
	Novice/Apprentice	**Apprentice/Practitioner**	**Practitioner/Expert**

THE CORE DECONSTRUCTED

RL.2.6 Acknowledge differences in the points of view of characters, including speaking in a different voice for each character when reading dialogue.

	REMEMBER/ UNDERSTAND	APPLY/ANALYZE	EVALUATE/CREATE
Factual Knowledge Dimension	Students can **explain** the meaning of specific terminology: *acknowledge, difference, point of view, character, voice, dialogue (and other Tier 2 or 3 words related to the content or text)*	Students can **use** specific terminology: *acknowledge, difference, point of view, character, voice, dialogue (and other Tier 2 or 3 words related to the content or text)*	Students can **check** their use of specific terminology: *acknowledge, difference, point of view, character, voice, dialogue (and other Tier 2 or 3 words related to the content or text)*
Conceptual Knowledge Dimension	Students can **identify** the differences in *point of view* between *characters* Students can **identify** the differences in *voice* between *characters*	Students can **organize** the information that contributes to characters' *point of view* Students can **organize** the information that contributes to characters' *voice*	Students can **generate** the connection between *voice* and *point of view*
Procedural Knowledge Dimension	Students know how to **explain** the process used to *acknowledge* Students know how to **infer** *voice* patterns of different *characters* when reading aloud	Students know how to **use** the process of *acknowledging* to change the *characters' voice*	Students know how to **monitor** *voice* patterns
Metacognitive Knowledge Dimension	Students are able to **recall** the details of the terms and concepts	Students are able to **select** relevant information to complete a task	Students are able to **judge** the details in their work for self-correction

                    Novice/Apprentice   **Apprentice/Practitioner**   **Practitioner/Expert**

THE CORE DECONSTRUCTED

RL.3.6 Distinguish their own point of view from that of the narrator or those of the characters.

	REMEMBER/ UNDERSTAND	APPLY/ANALYZE	EVALUATE/CREATE
Factual Knowledge Dimension	Students can **exemplify** the meaning of specific terminology: *distinguish, point of view, narrator, character* (and other Tier 2 or 3 words related to the content or text)	Students can **use** specific terminology: *distribute, point of view, narrator, character* (and other Tier 2 or 3 words related to the content or text)	Students can **check** their use of specific terminology: *distribute, point of view, narrator, character* (and other Tier 2 or 3 words related to the content or text)
Conceptual Knowledge Dimension	Students can **contrast** the details between my *point of view* and the *narrator's or character's*	Students can **attribute** *biases in point of view* (their own and the narrator or character)	Students can **generate** the connection between the teller of a narrative and *point of view*
Procedural Knowledge Dimension	Students know how to **explain** the steps used to *distinguish*	Students know how to **use** the steps to *distinguish*	Students know how to **check** their use of the steps to *distinguish*
Metacognitive Knowledge Dimension	Students are able to **recall** the details of the terms and concepts	Students are able to **discriminate** ideas that are relevant from irrelevant to complete a task	Students are able to **judge** the details in their work for self-correction

       Novice/Apprentice Apprentice/Practitioner Practitioner/Expert

	THE CORE DECONSTRUCTED		
	RL.4.6 Compare and contrast the point of view from which different stories are narrated, including the difference between first- and third-person narrations.		
	REMEMBER/ UNDERSTAND	**APPLY/ANALYZE**	**EVALUATE/CREATE**
Factual Knowledge Dimension	Students can **exemplify** the meaning of specific terminology: *compare, contrast, point of view, first-, third-person narration (and other Tier 2 or 3 words related to the content or text)*	Students can **distinguish** the attributes of *compare/ contrast and first/third-person point of view (and other Tier 2 or 3 words related to the content or text)*	Students can **critique** the *similar* and *contrasting* details of a *first- and third-person narration (and other Tier 2 or 3 words related to the content or text)*
Conceptual Knowledge Dimension	Students can **classify** the attributes of *first and third person*	Students can **attribute** *attitudes* of the narrator to their *point of view* in a story	Students can **generate** a conclusion about the *similarities* and *differences* between *first- and third-person narration* of the same story
Procedural Knowledge Dimension	Students know how to **explain** the steps used to *compare* Students know how to **explain** the steps used to *contrast*	Students know how to **use** the steps to *compare* Students know how to **use** the steps to *contrast*	Students know how to **detect** the biases (or assumptions) in a *first- and third person narration*
Metacognitive Knowledge Dimension	Students are able to **recall** the details of the terms and concepts	Students are able to **discriminate** ideas that are relevant from irrelevant to complete a task	Students are able to **judge** the details in their work for self-correction
	Novice/Apprentice	Apprentice/Practitioner	Practitioner/Expert

THE CORE DECONSTRUCTED

RL.5.6 Describe how a narrator's or speaker's point of view influences how events are described.

	REMEMBER/ UNDERSTAND	**APPLY/ANALYZE**	**EVALUATE/CREATE**
Factual Knowledge Dimension	Students can **paraphrase** the meaning of specific terminology: *narrator, speaker, point of view, influence, event, describe (and other Tier 2 or 3 words related to the content or text)*	Students can **organize** the terms *narrator, speaker, point of view, influence, event, describe (and other Tier 2 or 3 words related to the content or text)* according to their relationships	Students can **design** a structure to help others see the relationships between *narrator, speaker, point of view, influence, event, describe (and other Tier 2 or 3 words related to the content or text)*
Conceptual Knowledge Dimension	Students can **explain** how assumptions *influence point of view*	Students can **attribute** *influences* over time's impact on *point of view* of a speaker or narrator	Students can **test** the parallels between an individual's *point of view* and how it *influences* their thoughts/beliefs
Procedural Knowledge Dimension	Students know how to **construct** a model that shows the structure of a *description*	Students know how to **use** a model to write a *description*	Students know how to **generate** a *descriptive* paradox *between point of view* and *influence of a speaker or narrator*
Metacognitive Knowledge Dimension	Students are able to **represent** the details required for completing the task	Students are able to **discriminate** ideas that are relevant from irrelevant to complete a task	Students are able to **judge** the details in their work for self-correction

        Novice/Apprentice   **Apprentice/Practitioner**   **Practitioner/Expert**

TCD Practice: Practice the complete deconstruction of a standard.

Write the selected standard.

_____
_____
_____
_____

	Remember/Understand	Apply/Analyze	Evaluate/Create
Factual Knowledge			
Conceptual Knowledge			
Procedural Knowledge			
Metacognitive Knowledge			

TCD Journal Response

Take a moment to journal your immediate insights after learning the process and studying the fully deconstructed standard on the previous page.

_____
_____
_____
_____
_____
_____
_____
_____
_____

Consider each cell in the deconstruction matrix to brainstorm student work products that would demonstrate proof of learning. (See page 84 for some ideas.) Please note that some work products may be repeated when appropriate.

Student Work Product Ideas

	Remember/Understand	Apply/Analyze	Evaluate/Create
Factual Knowledge			
Conceptual Knowledge			
Procedural Knowledge			
Metacognitive Knowledge			

TCD Journal Responses

Review A deconstructed standard along with the process for deconstructing to determine the similarities and differences between the Remember/Understand, Apply/Analyze and Evaluate/Create columns.

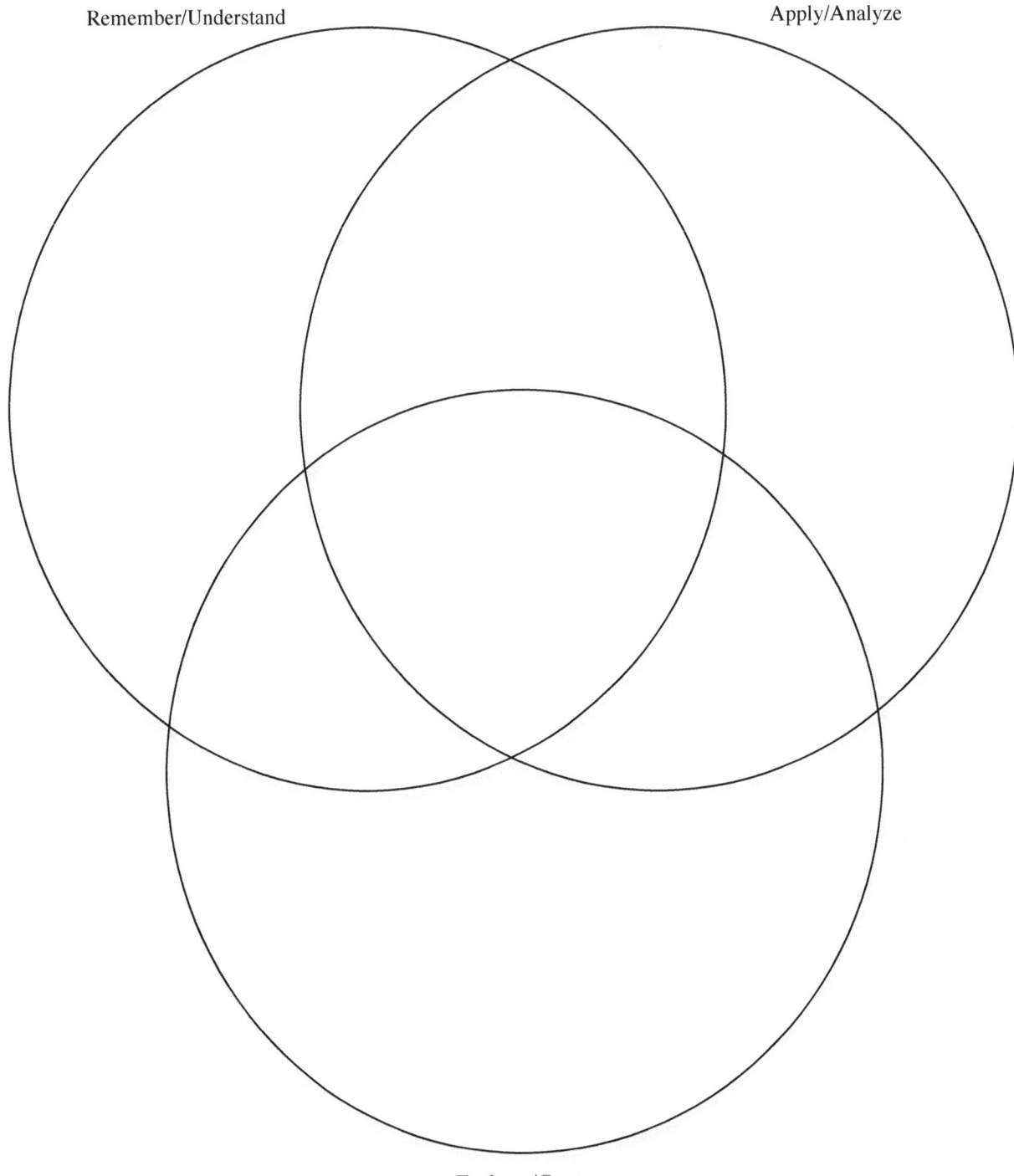

TCD Journal Responses

Review a deconstructed standard along with the process for deconstructing to determine the similarities and differences between the factual and conceptual knowledge, and procedural and metacognitive knowledge.

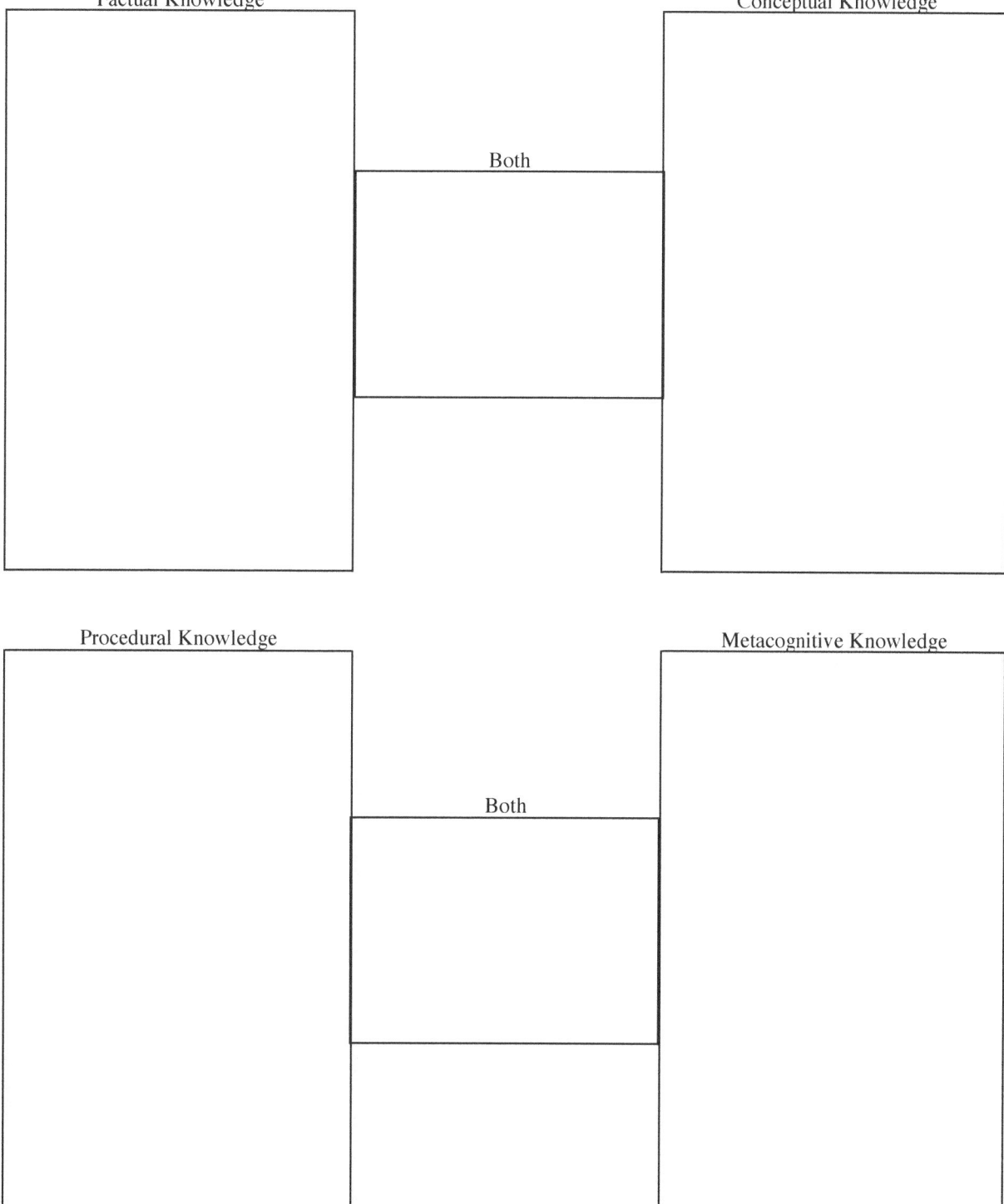

THE CORE DECONSTRUCTED

RI.K.3 With prompting and support, describe the connection between two individuals, events, ideas, or pieces of information in a text.

	REMEMBER/UNDERSTAND ALD 1, 2 & 3 | PLD 1 & 2	APPLY/ANALYZE ALD 3 & 4 | PLD 2 & 3	EVALUATE/CREATE ALD 4 | PLD 4 & 5
Factual Knowledge Dimension	Students can **illustrate** the meaning of specific terminology: *connection, individual, event, idea, piece, information, "piece of information"* (and other Tier 2 or 3 language found in text)	Students can **select** attributes of terminology: *connection, individual, event, idea, piece, information, "piece of information"* (and other Tier 2 or 3 language found in text)	Students can **coordinate** their use of specific terminology: *connection, individual, event, idea, piece, information, "piece of information"* (and other Tier 2 or 3 language found in text)
Conceptual Knowledge Dimension	Students can **recognize** similar details between two *individuals*	Students can **attribute** classification of *individuals* to details	Students can **produce** a generalization about two connected *individuals*
	Students can **recognize** similar details between two *events*	Students can **attribute** classification of *events* to details	Students can **produce** a generalization about two connected *events*
	Students can **recognize** similar details between two *ideas*	Students can **attribute** classification of *ideas* to details	Students can **produce** a generalization about two connected *ideas*
	Students can **recognize** similar details between two *pieces of information*	Students can **attribute** classification of *pieces of information* to details	Students can **produce** a generalization about two connected *pieces of information*
Procedural Knowledge Dimension	Students know how to **tell** the elements of a *description*	Students know how to **apply** the elements of *description*	Students know how to **generate** a descriptive piece on the connections
Metacognitive Knowledge Dimension	Students can **recall** the details of the assignment and how to receive support	Students are able to **ask** for directions that are relevant to completing a task	Students are able to **monitor** patterns in their behavior when support is needed
	Novice/Apprentice	Apprentice/Practitioner	Practitioner/Expert

TCD Practice: Practice deconstructing for **Factual Knowledge** with this standard.

Remember/Understand:

_____
_____
_____

Apply/Analyze:

_____
_____
_____

Evaluate/Create:

_____
_____
_____

THE CORE DECONSTRUCTED

RI.1.3 Describe the connection between two individuals, events, ideas, or pieces of information in a text.

	REMEMBER/UNDERSTAND ALD 1, 2 & 3 | PLD 1 & 2	APPLY/ANALYZE ALD 3 & 4 | PLD 2 & 3	EVALUATE/CREATE ALD 4 | PLD 4 & 5
Factual Knowledge Dimension	Students can **exemplify** the meaning of specific terminology: *connection, individual, event, idea, piece, information, "piece of information"* (and other Tier 2 or 3 language found in text)	Students can **organize** details based on terminology: *connection, individual, event, idea, piece, information, "piece of information"* (and other Tier 2 or 3 language found in text)	Students can **coordinate** their use of specific terminology: *connection, individual, event, idea, piece, information, "piece of information"* (and other Tier 2 or 3 language found in text)
Conceptual Knowledge Dimension	Students can **classify** two (or more) *individuals* by attributes	Students can **discriminate** features between connected and non-connected *individuals*	Students can **produce** a generalization on the connection between *two individuals*
	Students can **classify** two (or more) *ideas* by attributes	Students can **discriminate** features between connected and non-connected *ideas*	Students can **produce** a generalization on the connection between *two events*
	Students can **classify** two (or more) *events* by attributes	Students can **discriminate** features between connected and non-connected *events*	Students can **produce** a generalization on the connection between *two ideas*
	Students can **classify** two (or more) *pieces of information* by details	Students can **discriminate** features between connected and non-connected pieces of *information*	Students can **produce** a generalization on the connection between *two pieces of information*
Procedural Knowledge Dimension	Students know how to **explain** the elements of a *description*	Students know how to **apply** the elements of *description* in writing	Students know how to **generate** a descriptive piece on the connections
Metacognitive Knowledge Dimension	Students can **recall** the details of the assignment	Students are able to **discriminate** ideas that are relevant from irrelevant to complete a task	Students are able to **check** the details in their work for self-correction

Novice/Apprentice   Apprentice/Practitioner   Practitioner/Expert

TCD Practice: Practice deconstructing for **Factual Knowledge** with this standard.

Remember/Understand:

_____
_____
_____
_____

Apply/Analyze:

_____
_____
_____
_____

Evaluate/Create:

_____
_____
_____
_____

THE CORE DECONSTRUCTED

RI.2.3 Describe the connection between a series of historical events, scientific ideas or concepts, or steps in technical procedures in a text.

	REMEMBER/UNDERSTAND ALD 1, 2 & 3 | PLD 1 & 2	APPLY/ANALYZE ALD 3 & 4 | PLD 2 & 3	EVALUATE/CREATE ALD 4 | PLD 4 & 5
Factual Knowledge Dimension	Students can **exemplify** the meaning of specific terminology: *connection, historical, event, scientific, idea, concept, technical, procedure, series, steps* (and Tier 2 or 3 language found in text)	Students can **organize** details based on terminology: *connection, historical, event, scientific, idea, concept, technical, procedure, series, steps* (and Tier 2 or 3 language found in text)	Students can **plan** to write using specific information on *connection, historical, event, scientific, idea, concept, technical, procedure, series, steps* (and Tier 2 or 3 language found in text)
Conceptual Knowledge Dimension	Students can **compare** the origins of *historical events* Students can **compare** relationships between *scientific ideas* Students can **infer** recurring patterns in *technical procedures*	Students can **attribute** steps to the connections in *historical events* Students can **attribute** steps to the connections in *scientific ideas* Students can **attribute** steps to the connections in *technical procedures*	Students can **generalize** the connection between a series of steps and *historical events, scientific ideas or concepts, technical procedures*
Procedural Knowledge Dimension	Students know how to **explain** the features of a *description*	Students know how to **apply** the elements of *description* in writing	Students know how to **generate** a descriptive piece on the connections
Metacognitive Knowledge Dimension	Students can **recall** the details of the assignment	Students are able to **discriminate** ideas that are relevant from irrelevant to complete a task	Students are able to **monitor** the details in their work for self-correction
	Novice/Apprentice	Apprentice/Practitioner	Practitioner/Expert

TCD Practice: Practice deconstructing for **Factual Knowledge** with this standard.

Remember/Understand:

_____
_____
_____
_____

Apply/Analyze:

_____
_____
_____
_____

Evaluate/Create:

_____
_____
_____
_____

THE CORE DECONSTRUCTED

RI.3.3 Describe the relationship between a series of historical events, scientific ideas or concepts, or steps in technical procedures in a text, using language that pertains to time, sequence, and cause and effect.

	REMEMBER/UNDERSTAND ALD 1, 2 & 3 | PLD 1 & 2	APPLY/ANALYZE ALD 3 & 4 | PLD 2 & 3	EVALUATE/CREATE ALD 4 | PLD 4 & 5
Factual Knowledge Dimension	Students can **paraphrase** the meaning of specific terminology: *relationship, historical, event, scientific, idea, concept, technical, procedure, sequence (and Tier 2 or 3 language found in text)*	Students can **use** specific terminology: *relationship, historical, event, scientific, idea, concept, technical, procedure, sequence (and Tier 2 or 3 language found in text)*	Students can **detect** specific information on *events, procedures, ideas or concepts* in *historical, scientific* or *technical* text
Conceptual Knowledge Dimension	Students can **classify** *historical events* by *time* period Students can **explain** connections between *scientific ideas* Students can **recognize** a recurring patterns in *technical procedures*	Students can **differentiate** *historical events* by time period Students can **organize** the aspects of *scientific ideas or concepts* Students can **find coherence** in patterns in *technical procedures*	Students can **produce** a generalization about the relationship *between historical events and time; scientific ideas or concepts and cause and effect; technical procedures and series or sequence*
Procedural Knowledge Dimension	Students know how to **explain** the features of a *description* Students know how to **locate** the language that refers to *time; sequence or series; cause and effect*	Students know how to **use** the elements of *description* Students know how to **organize** specific *language* that refers to *time, sequence, or cause and effect*	Students know how to **generate** a descriptive relationship piece Students know how to **monitor** use of specific *language* that refers to *time, sequence or cause and effect*
Metacognitive Knowledge Dimension	Students can **recall** the details of the assignment	Students are able to **discriminate** ideas that are relevant from irrelevant to complete a task	Students are able to **judge** the details in their work for self-correction
	Novice/Apprentice	Apprentice/Practitioner	Practitioner/Expert

TCD Practice: Practice deconstructing for **Factual Knowledge** with this standard.

Remember/Understand:

_____

_____

_____

_____

Apply/Analyze:

_____

_____

_____

_____

Evaluate/Create:

_____

_____

_____

_____

THE CORE DECONSTRUCTED

RI.4.3 Explain events, procedures, ideas or concepts in a historical, scientific, or technical text, including what happened and why, based on specific information in the text.

	REMEMBER/UNDERSTAND ALD 1, 2 & 3 | PLD 1 & 2	APPLY/ANALYZE ALD 3 & 4 | PLD 2 & 3	EVALUATE/CREATE ALD 4 | PLD 4 & 5
Factual Knowledge Dimension	Students can **exemplify** the meaning of specific terminology: *explain, event, procedure, idea, concept, historical, scientific, technical, specific, information* (and other Tier 2 or 3 words related to the content or text)	Students can **use** specific terminology (*event, procedure, ideas or concepts*) when referring to disciplinary (*historical, scientific or technical*) text	Students can **detect** specific information on *events, procedures, ideas or concepts* in *historical, scientific or technical* text
Conceptual Knowledge Dimension	Students can **recognize** patterns of *cause and effect* in *events* in *historical* text	Students can **outline** *cause and effect* patterns in events in *historical* text	Students can **hypothesize** about trends in *events* in *historical* text
	Students can **recognize** patterns of *cause and effect* in *concepts* or *ideas* in *scientific* text	Students can **structure** the patterns in *concepts* or *ideas* in *scientific* text	Students can **hypothesize** about patterns in *ideas or concepts* in *scientific* text
	Students can **recognize** patterns of *cause and effect* in *procedures* in *technical* text	Students can **find coherence** in *procedures* in *technical* text	Students can **hypothesize** about general tendencies in *procedures* in *technical* text
Procedural Knowledge Dimension	Students know how to **illustrate** the elements of a well-structured text-based *explanation*	Students know how to **distinguish** the elements of a well-structured text-based *explanation*	Students know how to **critique** a well-structured text-based explanation
Metacognitive Knowledge Dimension	Students are able to **retrieve** specific information from *historical, scientific or technical* text	Students are able to **organize** specific information from *historical, scientific or technical* text	Students are able to **make judgments** while detecting, hypothesizing, and critiquing to self-correct
	Novice/Apprentice	Apprentice/Practitioner	Practitioner/Expert

TCD Practice: Practice deconstructing for **Factual Knowledge** with this standard.

Remember/Understand:

_____
_____
_____

Apply/Analyze:

_____
_____
_____

Evaluate/Create:

_____
_____
_____

THE CORE DECONSTRUCTED

RI.5.3 Explain the relationships or interactions between two or more individuals, events, ideas, or concepts in a historical, scientific, or technical text based on specific information in the text.

	REMEMBER/UNDERSTAND ALD 1, 2 & 3 | PLD 1 & 2	APPLY/ANALYZE ALD 3 & 4 | PLD 2 & 3	EVALUATE/CREATE ALD 4 | PLD 4 & 5
Factual Knowledge Dimension	Students can **exemplify** the meaning of specific terminology: *explain, relationship, interaction, individual, event, idea, concept, historical, scientific, technical (and other Tier 2 or 3 words related to the content or text)*	Students can **differentiate** the *relationships* or *interactions* between *individuals, events, ideas* or *concepts* in *historical, scientific* or *technical* text	Students can **monitor** the trends in *relationships* or *interactions* between *individuals, events, ideas* or *concepts* in *historical, scientific* or *technical* text
Conceptual Knowledge Dimension	Students can **contrast** the characteristics of *historical, scientific or technical text*	Students can **deconstruct** a *historical, scientific or technical* text for its essential elements	Students can **generate** the parallels between *historical, scientific or technical* text based on their essential elements
	Students can **identify** the interactions or relationships between *individuals, events, ideas or concepts* in text	Students can **outline** the interactions or relationships between *individuals, events, ideas or concepts* in text	Students can **generate** conclusions about *interactions* or *relationships* between *individuals, events, ideas or concepts* in text
Procedural Knowledge Dimension	Students know how to **illustrate** the elements of a well-structured text-based *explanation*	Students know how to **distinguish** a well-structured *explanation* text-based on it elements	Students know how to **critique** a well-structured text-based explanation
Metacognitive Knowledge Dimension	Students are able to **retrieve** specific information from *historical, scientific or technical text*	Students are able to **organize** specific information from *historical, scientific or technical text*	Students are able to **make judgments** while monitoring, generating, and critiquing to self-correct

Novice/Apprentice   Apprentice/Practitioner   Practitioner/Expert

TCD Practice: Practice deconstructing for **Factual Knowledge** with this standard.

Remember/Understand:

Apply/Analyze:

Evaluate/Create:

What About Standards with Multiple Indicators?

Multiple indicators accompany some standards. They tend to be the Writing, a few Speaking and Listening and Language standards. For those, the process is modified slightly in the following ways:

1. Delete the deconstruction step for the appropriate cognitive process column and procedural row to replace it with the indicators. (See step 8 to the right.)
2. Continue deconstructing for the other columns as usual.

Simple!
The sample deconstructed standards for Writing, Speaking and Listening, and/or Language that follow depict the additional steps.

Phase 1: Dissect the Standard (with the multiple indicators)

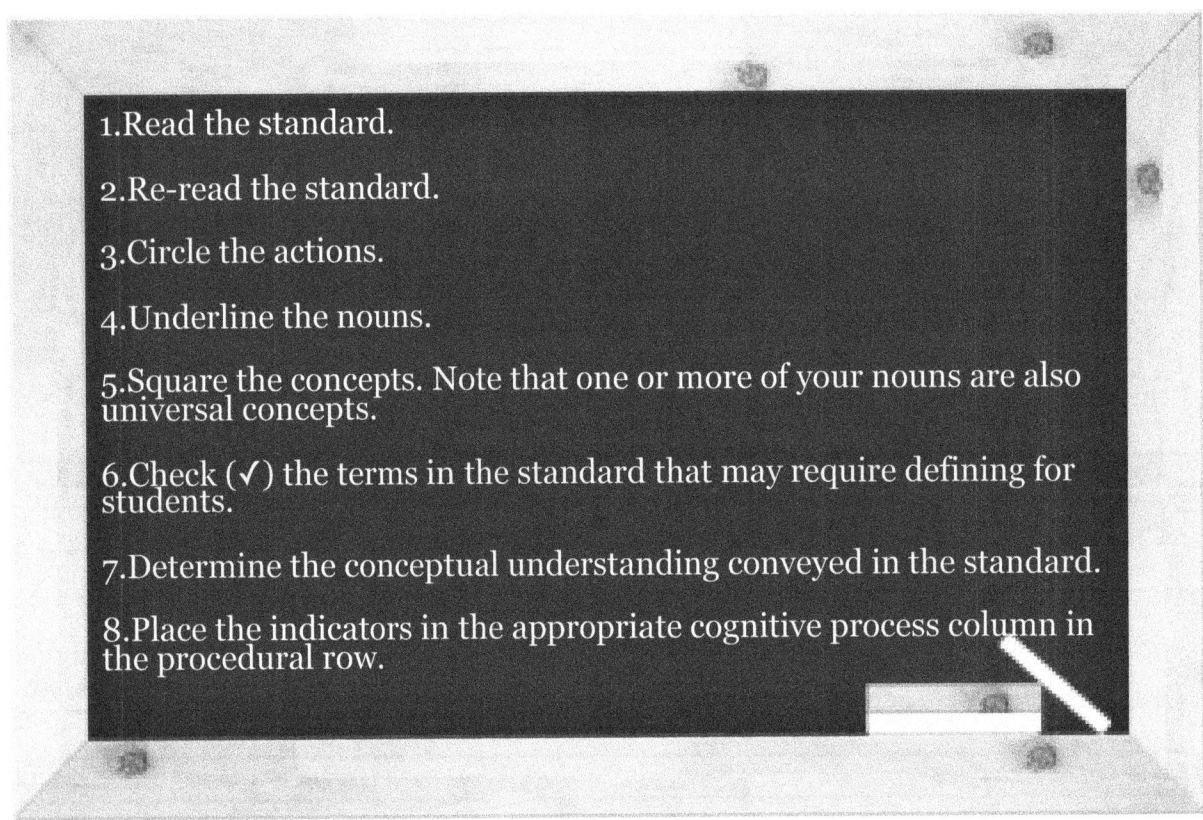

1. Read the standard.
2. Re-read the standard.
3. Circle the actions.
4. Underline the nouns.
5. Square the concepts. Note that one or more of your nouns are also universal concepts.
6. Check (✓) the terms in the standard that may require defining for students.
7. Determine the conceptual understanding conveyed in the standard.
8. Place the indicators in the appropriate cognitive process column in the procedural row.

Note: you may build up the standard for grades K-3 where the appropriate column tends to be Remember/Understand. Doing so advances your students' learning.

THE CORE DECONSTRUCTED

W.K.2 Use a combination of drawing, dictating and writing to compose informative/explanatory texts in which they name what they are writing about and supply some information about the topic.

	REMEMBER/UNDERSTAND ALD 1, 2 & 3 | PLD 1 & 2	APPLY/ANALYZE ALD 3 & 4 | PLD 2 & 3	EVALUATE/CREATE ALD 4 | PLD 4 & 5
Factual Knowledge Dimension	Students can **illustrate** the meaning of specific terminology: *explanatory, informative, topic, supply, information, compose, combination, dictating* (and other Tier 2 or 3 words related to the content or text)	Students can **select** visual representations of terminology: *explanatory, informative, topic, supply, information, compose, combination, dictating* (and other Tier 2 or 3 words related to the content or text)	Students can **design** a visual or written plan that demonstrates specific terminology: *explanatory, informative, topic, supply, information, compose, combination, dictating* (and other Tier 2 or 3 words related to the content or text)
Conceptual Knowledge Dimension	Students can **visually** exemplify the differences between *explaining and informing* (consider extending comparison to W.K.1 and W.K.3)	Students can **select** the *topic* and purpose of *informative/explanatory texts* based on information OR Students can **distinguish** between *explanatory and informative texts* based on information	Students can **produce** a general idea about *informative/explanatory* compositions
Procedural Knowledge Dimension	Students know how to **interpret** *dictated* information Students know how to verbally **summarize** relevant *information* *Supports RI.K.3	Students know how to **structure** *informative/explanatory information* based on *dictation*	Students know how to **compose** topic-based information for *informative/explanatory texts* in their own writing
Metacognitive Knowledge Dimension	Students are able to **recognize** the differences between *explaining and informing*	Students are able to **organize** details of *explanatory/informative text*	Students are able to **monitor** details for *explanatory/informative texts*

Novice/Apprentice   Apprentice/Practitioner   Practitioner/Expert

татCD Practice: Practice deconstructing for **Conceptual Knowledge** with this standard.

Remember/Understand:

_____
_____
_____
_____

Apply/Analyze:

_____
_____
_____
_____

Evaluate/Create:

_____
_____
_____
_____

THE CORE DECONSTRUCTED

W.1.2 Write informative/explanatory texts in which they name a topic, supply some facts about the topic, and provide some sense of closure.

	REMEMBER/UNDERSTAND ALD 1, 2 & 3 | PLD 1 & 2	APPLY/ANALYZE ALD 3 & 4 | PLD 2 & 3	EVALUATE/CREATE ALD 4 | PLD 4 & 5
Factual Knowledge Dimension	Students can **illustrate** the meaning of specific terminology: *explanatory, informative, topic, supply, facts, provide, closure (and other Tier 2 or 3 words related to the content or text)*	Students can **select** written representations of terminology: *explanatory, informative, topic, supply, facts, provide, closure (and other Tier 2 or 3 words related to the content or text)* Students can **differentiate** between *explanatory and informative; topic and facts*	Students can **check** for the rules in their writing based on specific terminology: *explanatory, informative, topic, supply, facts, provide, closure (and other Tier 2 or 3 words related to the content or text)*
Conceptual Knowledge Dimension	Students can **compare** the features of *informative and explanatory texts* (consider extending comparison to W. 1.1 and W.1.3)	Students can **find coherence** among *informative/explanatory texts'* elements *(topics, facts and closure)* in others' writing	Students can **judge** the structure of their *informative/explanatory texts* for *topic name, facts and closure*
Procedural Knowledge Dimension	Students know how to **classify** *topics in informative/explanatory texts* Students know how to **classify** *facts in informative/explanatory texts* Students know how to **explain** features of a *closure* *Supports RI.1.3	Students know how to **outline** *informative/explanatory texts'* elements in other's writing based *on topics, facts and closure*	Students know how to **generate** *informative/explanatory texts'* elements in their own writing *(topic name, facts and closure)*
Metacognitive Knowledge Dimension	Students are able to **recognize** elements in *explanatory/informative texts* such as *topic, facts and closure*	Students are able to **organize** elements from *explanatory/informative texts* such as *topic, facts and closure*	Students are able to **monitor** elements from *explanatory/informative texts* such as *topic, facts and closure*
	Novice/Apprentice	Apprentice/Practitioner	Practitioner/Expert

TCD Practice: Practice deconstructing for **Conceptual Knowledge** with this standard.

Remember/Understand:

_____
_____
_____
_____

Apply/Analyze:

_____
_____
_____
_____

Evaluate/Create:

_____
_____
_____
_____

THE CORE DECONSTRUCTED

W.2.2 Write informative/explanatory texts in which they introduce a topic, use facts and definitions to develop points, and provide a concluding statement or section.

	REMEMBER/UNDERSTAND ALD 1, 2 & 3 | PLD 1 & 2	APPLY/ANALYZE ALD 3 & 4 | PLD 2 & 3	EVALUATE/CREATE ALD 4 | PLD 4 & 5
Factual Knowledge Dimension	Students can **exemplify** the meaning of specific terminology: *explain, informative, introduce, topic, facts, definition, develop, points, conclude, statement and section*	Students can **select** representations of terminology: *explain, informative, introduce, topic, facts, definition, develop, points, conclude, statement and section* Students can **differentiate** between explanatory and informative; statement and section	Students can **design** a plan to *write informative/explanatory texts that introduce a topic, develop points with facts and definitions and provide a concluding statement*
Conceptual Knowledge Dimension	Students can **extrapolate** the patterns in *informative/explanatory texts'* elements *(introduction, development of points, concluding statement)*	Students can **find coherence** among *informative/explanatory texts'* elements *(introduction, development of points, concluding statement)*	Students can **coordinate** their text elements for *informing/explaining (introduction, development of points, concluding statement)*
Procedural Knowledge Dimension	Students know how to **classify** *informative/explanatory texts'* elements *(introduction, facts, details, development of points, concluding statement)* *Supports RI.2.3	Students know how to **outline** *informative/explanatory texts'* elements in other's writing *(introduction, facts, details, development of points, concluding statement)*	Students know how to **generate** *informative/explanatory texts'* elements in their own writing *(introduction, facts, details, development of points, concluding statement)*
Metacognitive Knowledge Dimension	Students are able to **recognize** elements in *explanatory/informative text such as introduction, facts, details, development of points, concluding statement*	Students are able to **organize** elements from *explanatory/informative texts such as introduction, facts, details, development of points, concluding statement*	Students are able to **monitor** elements from *explanatory/informative texts such as introduction, facts, details, development of points, concluding statement*
	Novice/Apprentice	Apprentice/Practitioner	Practitioner/Expert

TCD Practice: Practice deconstructing for **Conceptual Knowledge** with this standard.

Remember/Understand:

_____
_____
_____
_____

Apply/Analyze:

_____
_____
_____
_____

Evaluate/Create:

_____
_____
_____
_____

THE CORE DECONSTRUCTED

W.3.2 Write informative/explanatory texts to examine a topic and convey ideas and information clearly.

	REMEMBER/UNDERSTAND ALD 1, 2 & 3 | PLD 1 & 2	APPLY/ANALYZE ALD 3 & 4 | PLD 2 & 3	EVALUATE/CREATE ALD 4 | PLD 4 & 5
Factual Knowledge Dimension	Students can **exemplify** the meaning of specific terminology: *explain, informative, convey, examine, statement, section and paragraph*	Students can **use** the meaning of terminology: *explain, informative, convey, examine, statement, section and paragraph* Students can **differentiate** between explanatory and informative; paragraph and section	Students can **create** a plan to *write informative/explanatory text that examines a topic and conveys ideas and information*
Conceptual Knowledge Dimension	Students can **infer** the relationships between *introduction, clarity, linking words, grouping ideas and conclusions* in writing	Students can **select** the features that render ideas in *informative/explanatory texts clear and grouped in various sections* of writing	Students can **judge** the *cohesion* of their text for *clarity* and appropriate *related ideas* in all sections of their writing

Procedural Knowledge Dimension	Students know how to **classify** the elements of a text for:
	a. Topic introduction with
	  -Related information grouped together
	  -Illustrations' and usefulness in aiding comprehension
	b. Relevant topic content such as facts, definitions and details
	c. Ideas that connect within categories through linking words
	d. Conclusion-oriented statements, or sections
	
	*Supports RI.3.3
		Students know how to **analyze** information in other's writing for:
		a. Topic introduction with
		  -Related information grouped together
		  -Illustrations' and usefulness in aiding comprehension
		b. Relevant topic content such as facts, definitions and details
		c. Ideas that connect within categories through linking words
		d. Conclusion-oriented statements, or sections
			Students know how to:
			a. **Generate** a topic introduction
			  -Group related information together
			  -Include illustrations when useful to aiding comprehension
			b. **Develop** a topic with facts, definitions, and details
			c. **Link** ideas within categories using linking words and phrases
			d. **Generate** a concluding statement or section

Metacognitive Knowledge Dimension	Students are able to **recognize** elements in *explanatory/informative text such as introduction, grouped ideas, linking words, details and concluding statements or sections*	Students are able to **organize** elements from *explanatory/informative text such as introduction, grouped ideas, linking words, details and concluding statements or sections*	Students are able to **monitor** elements from *explanatory/informative text such as introduction, grouped ideas, linking words, details and concluding statements or sections*
	Novice/Apprentice	Apprentice/Practitioner	Practitioner/Expert

TCD Practice: Practice deconstructing for **Conceptual Knowledge** with this standard.

Remember/Understand:

Apply/Analyze:

Evaluate/Create:

THE CORE DECONSTRUCTED

W.4.2 Write informative/explanatory texts to examine a topic and convey ideas and information clearly.

	REMEMBER/UNDERSTAND ALD 1, 2 & 3 | PLD 1 & 2	APPLY/ANALYZE ALD 3 & 4 | PLD 2 & 3	EVALUATE/CREATE ALD 4 | PLD 4 & 5
Factual Knowledge Dimension	Students can **exemplify** the meaning of specific terminology: *explain, informative, convey, examine, statement, section, paragraph, format, domain-specific*	Students can **use** the meaning of terminology: *examine, formatting, illustrations, domain-specific, convey and idea or information* Students can **differentiate** between explanatory and informative; paragraph and section	Students can **create** a plan to *write informative/explanatory texts that examine a topic and conveys ideas and information*
Conceptual Knowledge Dimension	Students can **infer** the relationships between *clarity, grouping and ideas* in writing	Students can **select** the features that render ideas in *informative/explanatory texts clear and grouped*	Students can **coordinate** their *ideas* for *clarity* and appropriate *classifications*

Procedural Knowledge Dimension	Students know how to **classify** the elements of a text for:
	a. Topic introduction with
	   -Information grouped by paragraphs and sections
	   -Formatting, illustrations and multimedia's usefulness
	b. Relevant topic content such as facts, concrete details, quotations, etc.
	c. Ideas that connect within categories
	d. Precise and domain-specific language
	e. Conclusion-oriented statements or sections
	
	*Supports RI.4.3
		Students know how to **analyze** information in others' writing for:
		a. Topic introduction with
		   -Information grouped by paragraphs and sections
		   -Formatting, illustrations and multimedia's usefulness
		b. Relevant topic content such as facts, concrete details, quotations, etc.
		c. Ideas that connect within categories
		d. Precise and domain-specific language
		e. Conclusion-oriented statements, or sections
			Students know how to:
			a. **Generate** a clear topic introduction
			   -Group related information in paragraphs and sections
			   -Include formatting, illustrations, and multimedia when useful to aiding comprehension
			b. **Develop** a topic with facts, definitions, concrete details, quotations, or other information and examples related to the topic
			c. **Link** ideas within categories of information using words and phrases
			d. **Evaluate** their use of precise language and domain-specific vocabulary to inform about or explain the topic
			e. **Generate** a concluding statement or section related to the information or explanation presented

Metacognitive Knowledge Dimension	Students are able to **recognize** elements in *explanatory/informative texts such as introduction, relevant content, linked ideas, precise language, and concluding statements or sections*	Students are able to **organize** elements from *explanatory/informative text such as introduction, relevant content, linked ideas, precise language, and concluding statements or sections*	Students are able to **monitor** elements from *explanatory/informative texts such as introduction, relevant content, linked ideas, precise language, and concluding statements or sections* in their writing
	Novice/Apprentice	Apprentice/Practitioner	Practitioner/Expert

TCD Practice: Practice deconstructing for **Conceptual Knowledge** with this standard.

Remember/Understand:

_____
_____
_____

Apply/Analyze:

_____
_____
_____

Evaluate/Create:

_____
_____
_____

THE CORE DECONSTRUCTED

W.5.2 Write informative/explanatory texts to examine a topic and convey ideas and information clearly.

	REMEMBER/UNDERSTAND ALD 1, 2 & 3 | PLD 1 & 2	APPLY/ANALYZE ALD 3 & 4 | PLD 2 & 3	EVALUATE/CREATE ALD 4 | PLD 4 & 5
Factual Knowledge Dimension	Students can **exemplify** the meaning of specific terminology: *explain, informative, convey, observation, statement, section, logical, format, domain-specific*	Students can **use** the meaning of terminology: *logical, formatting, illustrations, domain-specific, convey and observation* Students can **differentiate** between explanatory and informative; statement and section	Students can **create** a plan to *write informative/explanatory text that examines a topic and conveys ideas and information*
Conceptual Knowledge Dimension	Students can **infer** the relationships between *clarity, focus, logic and ideas* in writing	Students can **select** the language that renders ideas in *informative/explanatory texts clear, focused, and logical*	Students can **coordinate** their *ideas* for *clarity, focus and logic*

Procedural Knowledge Dimension	Students know how to **classify** the elements of a text for:
	a. Topic introduction with
	   -General observation and focus
	   -Logically grouped information
	   -Formatting, illustrations and multimedia's usefulness
	b. Relevant topic content such as facts, concrete details, quotations, etc.
	c. Ideas that connect within and across categories
	d. Precise and domain-specific language
	e. Conclusion-oriented statement or sections
	
	*Supports RI.5.3
		Students know how to **analyze** information in other's writing for:
		a. Topic introduction with
		   -General observation and focus
		   -Logically grouped information
		   -Formatting, illustrations and multimedia's usefulness
		b. Relevant topic content such as facts, concrete details, quotations, etc.
		c. Ideas that connect within and across categories
		d. Precise and domain-specific language
		e. Conclusion-oriented statements or sections
			Students know how to:
			a. **Generate** a clear a topic introduction
			   -Provide general observation and focus
			   -Group related information logically
			   -Include formatting, illustrations, and multimedia when useful to aiding comprehension
			b. **Develop** a topic with facts, definitions, concrete details, quotations, or other information and examples related to the topic
			c. **Link** ideas within and across categories of information using words, phrases, and clauses
			d. **Evaluate** their use of precise language and domain-specific vocabulary to inform about or explain the topic
			e. **Generate** a concluding statement or section related to the information or explanation presented

Metacognitive Knowledge Dimension	Students are able to **recognize** elements in explanatory/informative text such as *introduction, relevant content, linked ideas, precise language, and concluding statements or sections*	Students are able to **organize** elements from explanatory/informative text such as *introduction, relevant content, linked ideas, precise language, and concluding statements or sections*	Students are able to **monitor** elements from explanatory/informative text such as *introduction, relevant content, linked ideas, precise language, and concluding statements or sections* in their writing

        Novice/Apprentice   Apprentice/Practitioner   Practitioner/Expert

TCD Practice: Practice deconstructing for **Conceptual Knowledge** with this standard.

Remember/Understand:

_____
_____
_____
_____

Apply/Analyze:

_____
_____
_____
_____

Evaluate/Create:

_____
_____
_____
_____

	THE CORE DECONSTRUCTED			
	SL.K.4 Describe familiar people, places, things and events and with prompting and support, provide additional detail.			
	REMEMBER/UNDERSTAND ALD 1, 2 & 3 | PLD 1 & 2	**APPLY/ANALYZE** ALD 3 & 4 | PLD 2 & 3	**EVALUATE/CREATE** ALD 4 | PLD 4 & 5
Factual Knowledge Dimension	Students can **represent** the meaning of specific terminology: *describe, event, familiar, detail, (and other Tier 2 or 3 words related to the content or text)*	Students can **use** the meaning of specific terminology to complete task: *describe, event, familiar, detail, (and other Tier 2 or 3 words related to the content or text)*	Students can **construct** a model representing specific terminology: *describe, event, familiar, detail, (and other Tier 2 or 3 words related to the content or text)*
Conceptual Knowledge Dimension	Students can **label** the *details* of *familiar people, places, things and events*	Students can **organize** *familiar people, places, things and events* by the *details* provided	Students can **produce** a generalization about *details and familiar people, places, things and events*
Procedural Knowledge Dimension	Students know how to **recognize** the features of *people, places, things and events*	Students know how to **attribute** the features of a *familiar people, places, things and events* by the *details* provided	Students know how to **produce** the *details* of a *people, places, things and events in a description*
Metacognitive Knowledge Dimension	Students are able to **retrieve** the steps of task	Students are able to **focus** the attributes of *familiar people, places, things and events* by the *details* provided	Students are able to **monitor** the influence of *prompting and support*
	Novice/Apprentice	Apprentice/Practitioner	Practitioner/Expert

TCD Practice: Practice deconstructing for **Procedural Knowledge** with this standard.

Remember/Understand:

_____

_____

_____

_____

Apply/Analyze:

_____

_____

_____

_____

Evaluate/Create:

_____

_____

_____

_____

THE CORE DECONSTRUCTED

SL.1.4 Describe people, places, things and events with relevant details expressing ideas and feelings clearly.

	REMEMBER/UNDERSTAND ALD 1, 2 & 3 | PLD 1 & 2	APPLY/ANALYZE ALD 3 & 4 | PLD 2 & 3	EVALUATE/CREATE ALD 4 | PLD 4 & 5
Factual Knowledge Dimension	Students can **represent** the meaning of specific terminology: *describe, event, relevant, detail, express, idea, feelings, clearly* (and other Tier 2 or 3 words related to the content or text)	Students can **select** *relevant details, events, expression of ideas and feelings, and clarity* in a *description* (based on the understanding of the terms)	Students can **coordinate** *relevant details, events, expression of ideas and feelings, and clarity* in a *description* (based on the knowledge of the terms)
Conceptual Knowledge Dimension	Students can **summarize** the significance of *relevant details and expressing ideas and feelings clearly*	Students can **integrate** the features of *relevant details, expressed ideas and feelings and clarity* in a *description*	Students can **produce** a generalization about relationship between *relevant details, expressed ideas and feelings and clarity* in a *description*
Procedural Knowledge Dimension	Students know how to **explain** the elements of a *description of people, places, things and events*	Students know how to **organize** the elements of a *description of people, places, things and events*	Students know how to **produce** the elements of a *description of people, places, things and events*
Metacognitive Knowledge Dimension	Students are able to **recognize** the attributes of *relevant details, ideas, feelings and clarity*	Students are able to **focus** the attributes of *relevant details, ideas, feelings and clarity*	Students are able to **detect** the attributes of *relevant details, ideas, feelings and clarity* in *description*
	Novice/Apprentice	Apprentice/Practitioner	Practitioner/Expert

TCD Practice: Practice deconstructing for **Procedural Knowledge** with this standard.

Remember/Understand:

_____
_____
_____
_____

Apply/Analyze:

_____
_____
_____
_____

Evaluate/Create:

_____
_____
_____
_____

THE CORE DECONSTRUCTED

SL.2.4 Tell a story or recount an experience with appropriate facts and relevant, descriptive details, speaking audibly in coherent sentences.

	REMEMBER/UNDERSTAND ALD 1, 2 & 3	PLD 1 & 2	APPLY/ANALYZE ALD 3 & 4	PLD 2 & 3	EVALUATE/CREATE ALD 4	PLD 4 & 5
Factual Knowledge Dimension	Students can **exemplify** the meaning of specific terminology: *recount, experience, appropriate, fact, relevant, descriptive, detail, audible, coherent, sentence* (and other Tier 2 or 3 words related to the content or text)	Students can **outline** the elements of *(appropriate facts, relevant descriptive details, coherent sentences)* in a *story* or *recount* of an *experience*	Students can **coordinate** the elements of *(appropriate facts, relevant descriptive details, coherent sentences)* in a *story* or *recount* of an *experience*
Conceptual Knowledge Dimension	Students can **generalize** the impact of recurring elements of *appropriate facts, relevant descriptive details, speaking audibly and coherent sentences*	Students can **differentiate** the elements of *appropriate facts, relevant descriptive details, and coherent sentences* (from their opposites)	Students can **produce** a generalization about relationships between *appropriate facts, relevant descriptive details, speaking audibly and coherent sentences*
Procedural Knowledge Dimension	Students know how to **clarify** the elements in a *telling of a story or recount* of an *experience*	Students know how to **distinguish** the elements in a *telling of a story or recount* of an *experience*	Students know how to **produce** the elements in a *telling of a story or recount* of an *experience*
Metacognitive Knowledge Dimension	Students are able to **recognize** the attributes of *appropriate facts, relevant descriptive details, audible voice level, and sentence coherence*	Students are able to **focus** the attributes of *appropriate facts, relevant descriptive details, audible voice level, and sentence coherence* in a *story* or *recount* of an *experience*	Students are able to **detect** the elements of *appropriate facts, relevant descriptive details, audible voice level, and sentence coherence* in their *story* or *recount* of an *experience*
	Novice/Apprentice	Apprentice/Practitioner	Practitioner/Expert

TCD Practice: Practice deconstructing for **Procedural Knowledge** with this standard.

Remember/Understand:

_____

_____

_____

_____

Apply/Analyze:

_____

_____

_____

_____

Evaluate/Create:

_____

_____

_____

_____

THE CORE DECONSTRUCTED

SL.3.4 Report on a topic or text, tell a story, or recount an experience with appropriate facts and relevant, descriptive details, speaking clearly at an understandable pace.

	REMEMBER/UNDERSTAND ALD 1, 2 & 3 | PLD 1 & 2	APPLY/ANALYZE ALD 3 & 4 | PLD 2 & 3	EVALUATE/CREATE ALD 4 | PLD 4 & 5
Factual Knowledge Dimension	Students can **exemplify** the meaning of specific terminology: *report, recount, experience, appropriate, fact, relevant, details support, theme, pace, descriptive, clarity (and other Tier 2 or 3 words related to the content or text)*	Students can **outline** the elements of *(appropriate facts, relevant descriptive details, themes, pace, clarity)* in a report, story or recount of an experience	Students can **coordinate** the elements of *(appropriate facts, relevant descriptive details, main idea themes, pace, clarity)* in a report, story or recount of an experience
Conceptual Knowledge Dimension	Students can **generalize** the impact of recurring elements of *appropriate facts, relevant descriptive details, theme, clarity and pace*	Students can **organize** the elements of *appropriate facts, relevant descriptive details, theme, clarity and pace*	Students can **monitor** the relationships between the elements *appropriate facts, relevant descriptive details, theme, clarity and pace*
Procedural Knowledge Dimension	Students know how to **clarify** the elements in a *text or topic* based *report*	Students know how to **distinguish** the elements in a *text or topic* based *report*	Students know how to **produce** the elements in a *text or topic* based *report*
	Students know how to **clarify** the elements in a *telling of a story or recount of an experience*	Students know how to **distinguish** the elements in a *telling of a story or recount of an experience*	Students know how to **produce** the elements in a *telling of a story or recount of an experience*
Metacognitive Knowledge Dimension	Students are able to **recognize** the attributes of *appropriate facts, relevant descriptive details, clarity and pace*	Students are able to **focus** the attributes of *clarity, pace,* and *appropriate, descriptive,* and *relevant* facts and *details* in a report, story or recount	Students are able to **critique** the elements of *clarity, pace,* and *appropriate, descriptive,* and *relevant* facts and *details* in their report, story or recount

Novice/Apprentice   Apprentice/Practitioner   Practitioner/Expert

TCD Practice: Practice deconstructing for **Procedural Knowledge** with this standard.

Remember/Understand:

_____
_____
_____
_____

Apply/Analyze:

_____
_____
_____
_____

Evaluate/Create:

_____
_____
_____
_____

THE CORE DECONSTRUCTED

SL.4.4 Report on a topic or text, tell a story, or recount an experience in an organized manner, using appropriate facts and relevant, descriptive details to support main ideas or themes; speak clearly at an understandable pace.

	REMEMBER/UNDERSTAND ALD 1, 2 & 3 | PLD 1 & 2	APPLY/ANALYZE ALD 3 & 4 | PLD 2 & 3	EVALUATE/CREATE ALD 4 | PLD 4 & 5
Factual Knowledge Dimension	Students can **exemplify** the meaning of specific terminology: *report, recount, experience organize, appropriate, fact, relevant, support, main idea, theme, pace, descriptive, clarity (and other Tier 2 or 3 words related to the content or text)*	Students can **outline** the elements of *(organization, appropriate facts, relevant descriptive details, main idea themes, pace, clarity)* in a report, story or recount of an experience	Students can **coordinate** the elements of *(organization, appropriate facts, relevant descriptive details, main idea themes, pace, clarity)* in a report, story or recount of an experience
Conceptual Knowledge Dimension	Students can **generalize** the impact of recurring elements of *organization, appropriate facts, relevant descriptive details, theme, clarity and pace*	Students can **organize** the elements of *organization, appropriate facts, relevant descriptive details, theme, clarity and pace*	Students can **monitor** the relationships between the elements *organization, appropriate facts, relevant descriptive details, theme, clarity and pace*
Procedural Knowledge Dimension	Students know how to **clarify** the elements in a *text or topic* based *report*	Students know how to **distinguish** the elements in a *text or topic* based *report*	Students know how to **produce** the elements in a *text or topic* based *report*
	Students know how to **clarify** the elements in a *telling of a story or recount of an experience*	Students know how to **distinguish** the elements in a *telling of a story or recount of an experience*	Students know how to **produce** the elements in a *telling of a story or recount of an experience*
Metacognitive Knowledge Dimension	Students are able to **recognize** the attributes of *organization, appropriate facts, relevant descriptive details, clarity and pace*	Students are able to **focus** the attributes of *clarity, pace organization,* and *appropriate, descriptive,* and *relevant* facts and details in a *report, story or recount*	Students are able to **critique** the elements of *clarity, pace organization,* and *appropriate, descriptive,* and *relevant* facts and details in their *report, story* or *recount*
	Novice/Apprentice	Apprentice/Practitioner	Practitioner/Expert

TCD Practice: Practice deconstructing for **Procedural Knowledge** with this standard.

Remember/Understand:
_____
_____
_____
_____

Apply/Analyze:
_____
_____
_____
_____

Evaluate/Create:
_____
_____
_____
_____

THE CORE DECONSTRUCTED

SL.5.4 Report on a topic or text or present an opinion sequencing ideas logically and using appropriate facts and relevant, descriptive details to support main ideas or themes; speak clearly at an understandable pace.

	REMEMBER/UNDERSTAND ALD 1, 2 & 3 | PLD 1 & 2	APPLY/ANALYZE ALD 3 & 4 | PLD 2 & 3	EVALUATE/CREATE ALD 4 | PLD 4 & 5
Factual Knowledge Dimension	Students can **exemplify** the meaning of specific terminology: *report, present, sequence, logical, appropriate, themes, pace, descriptive, clarity* (and other Tier 2 or 3 words related to the content or text)	Students can **outline** the elements of *(logically sequenced ideas, facts, relevant details, descriptive details, main idea, theme)* in a report or presentation	Students can **coordinate** the elements *(logically sequenced ideas, facts, relevant details, descriptive details, main idea, theme)* for a report or presentation
Conceptual Knowledge Dimension	Students can **generalize** the impact of recurring elements of *sequence, theme, logic, clarity and pace* on a report or presentation	Students can **organize** the elements of *sequence, theme, logic, clarity and pace* on a report or presentation	Students can **monitor** the relationships between the elements *sequence, theme, logic, clarity and pace* on a report or presentation
Procedural Knowledge Dimension	Students know how to **clarify** elements in a *text* based *report* Students know how to **clarify** elements in a *topic* based *report* Students know how to **clarify** elements in an *opinion* based *presentation*	Students know how to **distinguish** the elements in a *text* based *report* Students know how to **distinguish** the elements in a *topic* based *report* Students know how to **distinguish** the elements in an *opinion* based *presentation*	Students know how to **produce** the elements in a *text* based *report* Students know how to **produce** the elements in a *topic* based *report* Students know how to **produce** the elements in an *opinion* based *presentation*
Metacognitive Knowledge Dimension	Students are able to **recognize** the structure of *logical sequence*	Students are able to **focus** the attributes of a *clear* and *logically sequenced* report or presentation	Students are able to **critique** the details in their *report* or *presentation* for *clarity, pace* and *logical sequenced* to self-correct
	Novice/Apprentice	Apprentice/Practitioner	Practitioner/Expert

TCD Practice: **Practice deconstructing for Procedural Knowledge with this standard.**

Remember/Understand:

_____
_____
_____
_____

Apply/Analyze:

_____
_____
_____
_____

Evaluate/Create:

_____
_____
_____
_____

THE CORE DECONSTRUCTED

L.K.4 Determine or clarify the meaning of unknown and multiple-meaning words and phrases based on *kindergarten reading and content*.

	REMEMBER/UNDERSTAND ALD 1, 2 & 3 | PLD 1 & 2	APPLY/ANALYZE ALD 3 & 4 | PLD 2 & 3	EVALUATE/CREATE ALD 4 | PLD 4 & 5
Factual Knowledge Dimension	Students can visually **illustrate** the meaning of specific terminology: *unknown, phrases, multiple-meaning words, inflection (and other Tier 2 or 3 words related to the content or text)*	Students can **use** the illustrations of specific terminology: *unknown, phrases, multiple-meaning words, inflection (and other Tier 2 or 3 words related to the content or text)*	Students can **check** their understanding of specific terminology: *unknown, phrases, flexible, multiple-meaning words, inflection (and other Tier 2 or 3 words related to the content or text)*
Conceptual Knowledge Dimension	Students can **explain** the details of how words work	Students can **differentiate** between the features of *multiple-meaning words* Students can **differentiate** between the features of *words and their inflections*	Students can **produce** a generalization about *multiple-meaning words* Students can **produce** a generalization about *inflections*
Procedural Knowledge Dimension	Students know how to **explain** the process of a. Identifying new meanings for familiar words b. Explaining the use of the most frequently occurring inflections and affixes	Students know how to **organize** unknown terms in text to: a. Use new meanings for familiar words and apply them accurately b. Use the most frequently occurring inflections and affixes	Students know how to: a. **Evaluate** their use of new meanings for familiar words and apply them accurately b. **Monitor** the use of sthe most frequently occurring inflections and affixes
Metacognitive Knowledge Dimension	Students are able to **recall** ways for determining or clarifying word meanings	Students are able to **focus** on the structure of a word for determining or clarifying word meanings	Students are able to **monitor** their patterns for determining or clarifying word meanings for improvement
	Novice/Apprentice	Apprentice/Practitioner	Practitioner/Expert

TCD Practice: Practice deconstructing for **Metacognitive Knowledge** with this standard.

Remember/Understand:

_____
_____
_____
_____

Apply/Analyze:

_____
_____
_____
_____

Evaluate/Create:

_____
_____
_____
_____

THE CORE DECONSTRUCTED

L.1.4 Determine or clarify the meaning of unknown and multiple-meaning words and phrases based on *grade 1 reading and content* choosing flexibly from a array of strategies.

	REMEMBER/UNDERSTAND ALD 1, 2 & 3 | PLD 1 & 2	APPLY/ANALYZE ALD 3 & 4 | PLD 2 & 3	EVALUATE/CREATE ALD 4 | PLD 4 & 5
Factual Knowledge Dimension	Students can visually **illustrate** in written form the meaning of specific terminology: *unknown, phrases, flexible, array, strategies, context, digital, inflection* (and other Tier 2 or 3 words related to the content or text)	Students can **use** the illustrations of specific terminology: : *unknown, phrases, flexible, array, strategies, context, digital, inflection* (and other Tier 2 or 3 words related to the content or text) Students can **differentiate** between the benefits of various *strategies*	Students can **check** their understanding of specific terminology: *unknown, phrases, flexible, strategies, context, digital, inflection* (and other Tier 2 or 3 words related to the content or text)
Conceptual Knowledge Dimension	Students can **explain** the elements of the *strategies for determining and clarifying the meaning of unknown and multiple-meaning words*	Students can **apply** the *strategies for determining and clarifying the meaning of unknown and multiple-meaning words*	Students can **produce** a generalization about the *strategies for determining and clarifying the meaning of unknown and multiple-meaning words*
Procedural Knowledge Dimension	Students know how to verbally **illustrate** the process of: a. Using sentence level context as a clue to the meaning of a word or phrase. b. Using frequently occurring affixes as a clue to the meaning of the word c. Identifying frequently occurring root words and their inflectional forms	Students know how to **organize** unknown terms in text to: a. Use sentence level context as a clue to the meaning of a word or phrase. b. Use frequently occurring affixes as a clue to the meaning of the word c. Apply knowledge of frequently occurring root words and their inflectional forms	Students know how to: a. **Evaluate** their use sentence level context as a clue to the meaning of a word or phrase. b. **Monitor** the use of frequently occurring affixes as a clue to the meaning of a word c. **Check** their application of frequently occurring root words and their inflectional forms
Metacognitive Knowledge Dimension	Students are able to **recall** strategies for determining or clarifying word meanings	Students are able to **focus** on the structure of a sentence for context to apply appropriate strategies	Students are able to **monitor** their patterns for determining or clarifying word meanings for improvement

Novice/Apprentice　　　　Apprentice/Practitioner　　　　Practitioner/Expert

TCD Practice: Practice deconstructing for **Metacognitive Knowledge** with this standard.

Remember/Understand:

_____
_____
_____
_____

Apply/Analyze:

_____
_____
_____
_____

Evaluate/Create:

_____
_____
_____
_____

THE CORE DECONSTRUCTED

L.2.4 Determine or clarify the meaning of unknown and multiple-meaning words and phrases based on *grade 2 reading and content* choosing flexibly from an array of strategies.

	REMEMBER/UNDERSTAND ALD 1, 2 & 3 | PLD 1 & 2	APPLY/ANALYZE ALD 3 & 4 | PLD 2 & 3	EVALUATE/CREATE ALD 4 | PLD 4 & 5
Factual Knowledge Dimension	Students can **interpret** the meaning of specific terminology: *unknown, phrases, flexible, array, strategies, context, digital, predict*	Students can **use** the interpretations of specific terminology: *unknown, phrases, flexible, array, strategies, context, digital, predict* Students can **differentiate** between the benefits of various *strategies*	Students can **judge** use of various *strategies* to determine or clarify meaning
Conceptual Knowledge Dimension	Students can **classify** the elements of *word parts*	Students can **find coherence** among *words parts and phrases*	Students can **produce** a generalization about impact of *words parts and phrases*
Procedural Knowledge Dimension	Students know how to **explain** the differences between: a. Using sentence level context as a clue to the meaning of a word or phrase. b. Carrying out the use of prefixes c. Using known root word as a clue to the meaning of an unknown word with the same root d. Using knowledge of the meaning of individual words to predict the meaning of compound words e. Using glossaries or beginning dictionaries, both print and digital, to determine or clarify the precise meaning of key words and phrases	Students know how to **organize** unknown terms in text to: a. Use sentence level context as a clue to the meaning of a word or phrase. b. Carry out the application of prefixes c. Use known root word as a clue to the meaning of an unknown word with the same root d. Use knowledge of the meaning of individual words to predict the meaning of compound words e. Use glossaries or beginning dictionaries, both print and digital, to determine or clarify the precise meaning of key words and phrases	Students know how to: a. **Evaluate** their use of sentence level context as a clue to the meaning of a word or phrase. b. **Determine** the meaning of the new word formed when a known prefix is added to a known word c. **Check** their use of known root word as a clue to the meaning of an unknown word with the same root d. **Check** their use of the meaning of individual words to predict the meaning of compound words e. **Create** a plan for using glossaries or beginning dictionaries, both print and digital, to determine or clarify the precise meaning of key words and phrases
Metacognitive Knowledge Dimension	Students are able to **recall** strategies for determining or clarifying word meanings	Students are able to **focus** on the structure of a sentence for context to apply appropriate strategies	Students are able to **monitor** their patterns for determining or clarifying word meanings for improvement
	Novice/Apprentice	Apprentice/Practitioner	Practitioner/Expert

TCD Practice: Practice deconstructing for **Metacognitive Knowledge** with this standard.

Remember/Understand:

Apply/Analyze:

Evaluate/Create:

THE CORE DECONSTRUCTED

L.3.4 Determine or clarify the meaning of unknown and multiple-meaning words and phrases based on *grade 3 reading and content* choosing flexibly from a range of strategies.

	REMEMBER/UNDERSTAND ALD 1, 2 & 3 | PLD 1 & 2	APPLY/ANALYZE ALD 3 & 4 | PLD 2 & 3	EVALUATE/CREATE ALD 4 | PLD 4 & 5
Factual Knowledge Dimension	Students can **interpret** the meaning of specific terminology: *unknown, phrases, flexible, strategies, context*	Students can **use** the interpretations of specific terminology: *unknown, phrases, flexible, strategies, context* Students can **differentiate** between the benefits of various *strategies*	Students can **judge** use of various *strategies* to determine or clarify meaning of terminology
Conceptual Knowledge Dimension	Students can **exemplify** the differences between the *strategies* for *determining and clarifying* meaning of unknown and multiple-meaning words and phrases	Students can **find coherence** between the *strategies* for *determining and clarifying* meaning of unknown and multiple-meaning words and phrases	Students can **design** a procedure for selecting the *strategies* for *determining and clarifying* meaning of unknown and multiple-meaning words and phrases
Procedural Knowledge Dimension	Students know how to **explain** the relationships among: a. Using sentence level context as a clue to the meaning of a word or phrase. b. Carrying out the use of affixes c. Use of known root word as a clue to the meaning of an unknown word with the same root d. Using glossaries or beginning dictionaries, both print and digital, to determine or clarify the precise meaning of key words and phrases	Students know how to **organize** unknown terms in text to: a. Use sentence level context as a clue to the meaning of a word or phrase. b. Carry out the application of affixes c. Use of known root word as a clue to the meaning of an unknown word with the same root d. Use glossaries or beginning dictionaries, both print and digital, to determine or clarify the precise meaning of key words and phrases	Students know how to: a. **Evaluate** their use of sentence level context as a clue to the meaning of a word or phrase. b. **Determine** the meaning of the new word formed when a known affix is added to a known word c. **Check** their use of known root word as a clue to the meaning of an unknown word with the same root d. **Create** a plan for using glossaries or beginning dictionaries, both print and digital, to determine or clarify the precise meaning of key words and phrases
Metacognitive Knowledge Dimension	Students are able to **recall** strategies for determining or clarifying word meanings	Students are able to **focus** on the structure of text for context and or words to apply appropriate strategies	Students are able to **monitor** their patterns for determining or clarifying word meanings for improvement
	Novice/Apprentice	Apprentice/Practitioner	Practitioner/Expert

TCD Practice: Practice deconstructing for **Metacognitive Knowledge** with this standard.

Remember/Understand:

_____
_____
_____
_____

Apply/Analyze:

_____
_____
_____
_____

Evaluate/Create:

_____
_____
_____
_____

THE CORE DECONSTRUCTED

L.4.4 Determine or clarify the meaning of unknown and multiple-meaning words and phrases based on *grade 4 reading and content* choosing flexibly from a range of strategies.

	REMEMBER/UNDERSTAND ALD 1, 2 & 3 | PLD 1 & 2	APPLY/ANALYZE ALD 3 & 4 | PLD 2 & 3	EVALUATE/CREATE ALD 4 | PLD 4 & 5
Factual Knowledge Dimension	Students can **interpret** the meaning of specific terminology: *unknown, phrases, flexible, strategies, context*	Students can **use** the interpretations of specific terminology: *unknown, phrases, flexible, strategies, context* Students can **differentiate** between the benefits of various *strategies*	Students can **judge** the use of various *strategies* to determine or clarify terminology
Conceptual Knowledge Dimension	Students can **exemplify** the relationships between *meaning, context and precision*	Students can **find coherence** between the ideas of *meaning, context and precision*	Students can **design** a procedure for using *context, precision and strategies* to determine or clarify meaning
Procedural Knowledge Dimension	Students know how to **explain** the relationships between: a. Context and meaning of words and phrases b. Affixes and meaning of words and phrases c. Reference materials and precision in determining or clarifying the meaning of unknown words and phrases	Students know how to **organize** unknown terms in text to: a. Use *context* as a clue to the *meaning* of a *word* or *phrase* b. Use common, grade-appropriate Greek and Latin affixes and roots as clues to the meaning of a word c. Consult reference materials both print and digital to: -find pronunciation -determine or clarify the precise meaning of key words and phrases	Students know how to: a. **Evaluate** their use of context as a clue to the meaning of a word or phrase b. **Detect** their use of common, grade-appropriate Greek and Latin affixes and roots as clues to the meaning of a word c. **Judge** their consultation of reference materials both print and digital to -find pronunciation -determine or clarify the precise meaning of key words and phrases
Metacognitive Knowledge Dimension	Students are able to **recall** strategies for determining or clarifying word meanings	Students are able to **focus** on the structure of text for context and or words to apply appropriate strategies	Students are able to **monitor** their patterns for determining or clarifying word meanings for improvement
	Novice/Apprentice	Apprentice/Practitioner	Practitioner/Expert

TCD Practice: Practice deconstructing for **Metacognitive Knowledge** with this standard.

Remember/Understand:

_____
_____
_____

Apply/Analyze:

_____
_____
_____

Evaluate/Create:

_____
_____
_____

THE CORE DECONSTRUCTED

L.5.4 Determine or clarify the meaning of unknown and multiple-meaning words and phrases based on *grade 5 reading and content* choosing flexibly from a range of strategies.

	REMEMBER/UNDERSTAND ALD 1, 2 & 3 | PLD 1 & 2	APPLY/ANALYZE ALD 3 & 4 | PLD 2 & 3	EVALUATE/CREATE ALD 4 | PLD 4 & 5
Factual Knowledge Dimension	Students can **interpret** the meaning of specific terminology: *unknown, phrases, flexible, strategies, context, precise (precision)*	Students can **use** the interpretations of [the specific terminology] (to determine or clarify meaning) Students can **differentiate** between the benefits of various *strategies*	Students can **judge** use of various *strategies* to determine or clarify meaning
Conceptual Knowledge Dimension	Students can **exemplify** the relationships between *meaning, context and precision*	Students can **find coherence** between the ideas of *meaning, context and precision*	Students can **design** a procedure for using *context, precision and strategies* to determine or clarify meaning
Procedural Knowledge Dimension	Students know how to **explain** the relationships between: a. Context and meaning of words and phrases b. Affixes and meaning of words and phrases c. Reference materials and precision in determining or clarifying the meaning of unknown words and phrases	Students know how to **organize** unknown terms in text to: a. Use *context* as a clue to the *meaning* of a *word* or *phrase* b. Use common, grade-appropriate Greek and Latin affixes and roots as clues to the meaning of a word c. Consult reference materials both print and digital to: -find pronunciation -determine or clarify the precise meaning of key words and phrases	Students know how to: a. **Evaluate** their use of context as a clue to the meaning of a word or phrase b. **Detect** their use of common, grade-appropriate Greek and Latin affixes and roots as clues to the meaning of a word c. **Judge** their consultation of reference materials both print and digital to -find pronunciation -determine or clarify the precise meaning of key words and phrases
Metacognitive Knowledge Dimension	Students are able to **recall** strategies for determining or clarifying word meanings	Students are able to **focus** on the structure of text for context and or words to apply appropriate strategies	Students are able to **monitor** their patterns for determining or clarifying word meanings for improvement
	Novice/Apprentice	Apprentice/Practitioner	Practitioner/Expert

TCD Practice: Practice deconstructing for **Metacognitive Knowledge** with this standard.

Remember/Understand:

_____
_____
_____
_____

Apply/Analyze:

_____
_____
_____
_____

Evaluate/Create:

_____
_____
_____
_____

TCD Practice: Practice the complete deconstruction of a standard.

Write the selected standard.

_____
_____
_____
_____
_____

	Remember/Understand	Apply/Analyze	Evaluate/Create
Factual Knowledge			
Conceptual Knowledge			
Procedural Knowledge			
Metacognitive Knowledge			

TCD Practice: Practice the complete deconstruction of a standard.

Write the selected standard.

_____
_____
_____
_____

	Remember/Understand	Apply/Analyze	Evaluate/Create
Factual Knowledge			
Conceptual Knowledge			
Procedural Knowledge			
Metacognitive Knowledge			

TCD Practice: Practice the complete deconstruction of a standard.

Write the selected standard.

_____
_____
_____
_____

	Remember/Understand	Apply/Analyze	Evaluate/Create
Factual Knowledge			
Conceptual Knowledge			
Procedural Knowledge			
Metacognitive Knowledge			

TCD Practice: Practice the complete deconstruction of a standard.

Write the selected standard.

_____
_____
_____
_____

	Remember/Understand	**Apply/Analyze**	**Evaluate/Create**
Factual Knowledge			
Conceptual Knowledge			
Procedural Knowledge			
Metacognitive Knowledge			

You are ready!

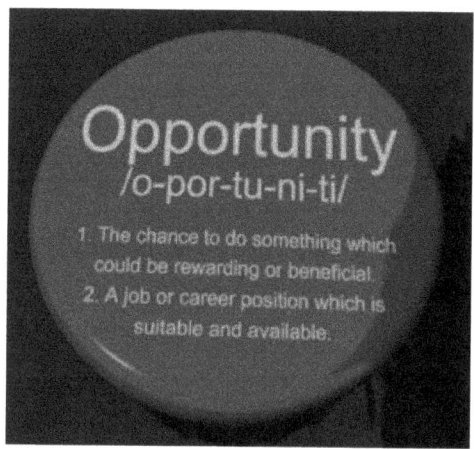

1. Continue deconstructing either by yourself or with your colleagues, and before long, you would have deconstructed every standard.

2. Continue to Chapter 3 for an example of how to design a comprehensive lesson using TCD.

TCD Journal Response

Now that you have deconstructed, consider answering one or more of the following reflection questions: What do you know now that you didn't before? What are you able to do better? How will you use the process? How will you use your deconstructed standard?

_____
_____
_____
_____
_____
_____
_____
_____
_____
_____

Chapter 3

Teaching the Standards

Writing is thinking. To write well is to think clearly. That's why it's so hard.

~David McCullough

Writing Robust Objectives. You may be asking, "Now that I've deconstructed the standards, now what?" *Now you design and teach!* Deconstructing provides a number of benefits for designing and teaching comprehensive lessons. You can:

1. Create pre-assessments using the apply/analyze column to determine the readiness for the majority of your students. If the majority of your students do well, consider a brief review then move forward to the evaluate/create column. If the majority do not do well, introduce the standard by starting with the remember/understand column.
2. Plan for your flexible groups by examining clusters. You may have 2 to 7 students who indicate similar needs either for enrichment or acceleration. Use the appropriate column or cell(s) to differentiate for your small groups.
3. Individualize your differentiation for students who show a specific need. Consider directing their tutors to that need, plan specialized assignments for class or home, or support the student during 1-on-1 conferencing in the area(s) they demonstrated needs.

Wherever you begin, remember that once your students are able to successfully perform throughout the full range of TCD, then they have truly mastered the standard.

After deciding how to move forward with your groups, it's time to design a lesson using the objective stems. The stems provide you with the starting place for writing a complete learning target or objective. A clear and complete learning objective entails the cognitive process, the DCI component, the content being taught, the resource being used to facilitate learning, the product of the students' thinking and the who of the learning. A tool that can support you in managing these components is referred to as the Objective Builder.

When applied appropriately, the Objective Builder allows students to have the clarity they require to perform at the level of expectations introduced by the teacher. Furthermore, the latter portion of the Objective Builder asks students to make their thinking visible by engaging in brief performance tasks--a skill the 21st century student needs.

Given that TCD includes the cognitive process and the DCI, you only need to complete the learning target with the remaining components of the Objective Builder, then move on to designing your well-aligned lesson.

Objective Builder

Structure of Objective: Students will <u>cognitive process</u> the <u>discipline domain</u> of <u>content focus</u> using <u>resource</u> to <u>product</u> in **group's size**.

COGNITIVE PROCESSES (Choose one)					
Remember (Retrieve relevant knowledge)	**Understand** (Construct meaning from instructional messages, including oral written and graphic communication)	**Apply** (Carry out or use a procedure in a given situation.)	**Analyze** (Break material into its constituent parts and determine how the parts relate to one another and to an overall structure or purpose)	**Evaluate** (Make judgments based on criteria and standards)	**Create** (Put elements together to form a coherent or functional whole; reorganize elements into a new pattern or structure)
Recognize, *identify*; **recall**, *retrieve*	**Interpret**, *clarify, paraphrase, represent, translate*; **exemplify**, *illustrate, instantiate*; **classify**, *categorize, subsume*; **infer**, *conclude, extrapolate, interpolate, predict*; **compare**, *contrast, map, match*; **explain**, *construct models*	**Execute**, *carry out*; **implement**, *use*	**Differentiate**, *discriminate, distinguish, focus, select*; **organize**, *find coherence, integrate, outline, parse, structure*; **attribute**, *deconstruct*	**Check**, *coordinate, detect, monitor, test*; **critique**, *judge*	**Generate**, *hypothesize*; **plan**, *design*; **produce**, *construct*
Novice/Apprentice		Apprentice/Practitioner		Practitioner/Expert	

DISCIPLINE DOMAINS (Choose one)					
Domain of Discipline Depth		**Domain of Discipline Complexity**		**Domain of Discipline Imperatives**	
Depth Choices	Descriptions	Complexity Choice	Descriptions	Imperative Choices	Descriptions
Language of the Discipline	Terms, nomenclature used by the disciplinarian or expert (or used within a discipline)	Change over Time	Past, present, future; across, during various time periods; change	Origin	The beginning, root, or source of an idea or event
Big Idea (Generalization, Principle, Theory, or Concept)	Broad conclusions based on evidence; rules based on tested and accepted facts or assumptions; basic truths, laws or assumptions	Multiple Perspectives	Differing points of view; opinions based on varied roles and responsibilities; attitudes when considering or viewing	Contribution	The significant part or result of an idea or event
Patterns	Designs, models, recurring elements, cycles, order, composite of characteristics	Across Disciplines	Connections, relationships within, between, and among various disciplines or subject areas	Convergence	The coming together or meeting point of events or ideas
Rules	Standards, organizational patterns, structure, order			Parallel	Ideas or events that are similar and can be compared to one another
Trends	Changes over time; general tendency of direction, drift; influences over time causing effects to happen			Paradox	The contradictory elements in an event or idea
Unanswered Questions	Knowledge yet to be discovered, explored, proven; unclear information needing further evidence or support				
Essential Details	Features, attributes, elements, specific information, elaboration, embellishment				
Ethics	Value-laden ideas, information; ideas opinions related to bias, prejudice, discrimination				

INSERT THE CONTENT FOCUS FROM YOUR DISCIPLINE (See your standards)

RESOURCES (Choose the appropriate resource[s])

Offline	Online
Textbook, photographs, magazine, newspaper, interview, student-created tools, or another named offline resource	Textbook, website, software, online encyclopedia, journal, article, or another named online resource

PRODUCT (Choose one from the desired category)

Visual	Display	Vocal	Multimedia	Written
Poster	Model	Debate	Web-page	Response to Literature
Drawing	Mobile	Panel Discussion	Illustrated Book	Report
Timeline	Diorama	Lesson	Voice Thread	Article
Diagram	Art Gallery	Report	Photo Essay	Persuasive Essay
Graphic Organizer	Museum Exhibit	Play	PowerPoint	Sequel
Map	Sculpture	Readers' Theater	Video Poetry	Letter
BitStrips	Twiddla	Talk Show	Blog	Critique
Book Cover	Blueprint	Monologue	Video Portfolio	Argument
Chart	Magazine Cover	Lecture	News Report	Character sketch
Photo Essay	Advance Organizer	Oral History	Animoto	Annotated Bibliography
Picture Dictionary	Calendar	Oral Report	Musical Composition	Book Review
Prezi	Glogster	Interview	Documentary	Story in New Genre
Other visual	Other display	Other vocal	Other media	Other writings

GROUP SIZE (Choose appropriately for task)

Individually	Dyad	Triad	Quad

Directions for Building Your Objective:
Build your lesson objective by selecting the most appropriate term from each of the 5 categories (thinking skill, discipline domain, resource, product and group size). Use your standards to determine the content focus from your discipline. Please note that the prepositions can be modified as needed.

Sample Objectives:
Students will explain their process for identifying who is talking in a text using their recording to write their explanation **individually**.
Adapted from CCSS RL.1.6: Identify who is telling the story at various points in a text.

Students will test the parallels between an individual's point of view and how it influences their description of events using Bread and Roses, Too to write a review **individually.**
Adapted from CCSS RL.5.6: Describe how a narrator or speaker's point of view influences how events are described.

Students will attribute the details of five characters points of view to the effects in the class text using their classification notes to generate a Voice Thread presentation with a **partner**.
Adapted from CCSS RL.8.6: Analyze how differences in the points of view of the characters and the audience or reader create such effects as suspense or humor.

Students will distinguish the details of point of view from actual statements in the course text using their close reading notes to draft an **individual** oral report on satire.
Adapted from CCSS RL.11-12.6: Analyze a case in which grasping point of view requires distinguishing what is directly stated in a text from what is really meant.

TCD Practice: What are the identifiable challenges with this learning objective?

Students will engage in a read aloud in order to assess the dangers of freedom.

_____
_____
_____
_____

"Poor lesson plans mean students learn poorly. And poor lesson plans, begin with poor learning goals or objectives. Effective lesson delivery begins with a well-conceived lesson design; the beginning of a well-conceived design is the objective; and the heart of an objective is the cognitive process. The cognitive processes in Bloom's Taxonomy are not simply verbs. They are the work you want the brain to engage in to result in a product of learning (Brown, 2012)."

TCD Practice: Use the objective stems from the TCDs on previous pages and follow the structure from the Objective Builder to practice.

Structure of Objective:
Students will **cognitive process** the **discipline domain** of **content focus** using **resource** to **product** in **group's size**.

Remember/Understand Practice:

_____
_____
_____
_____

Apply/Analyze Practice:

_____
_____
_____
_____

Evaluate/Create Practice:

_____
_____
_____
_____

Designing Robust Learning Experiences.

Past experience and feedback have shown that the first few applications of the **Objective Builder** are challenging, mainly because the DCI component is new to some teachers. Fortunately though, past experience has also demonstrated that repeated application yields to ease of use, improved instruction and increased student learning.

School leaders and teachers who use the tool tend to express the same sentiment, and that is, the process of using the **Objective Builder** generates the ideas for the lesson. Hence, learning goals become distinct from the learning activities, and the objective, instruction and assessment are all aligned, resulting in improved learning. In Heather's words,

> *"The biggest difference I have seen in my classrooms is at the metacognitive stage of learning. Student writing as well as reflective thinking are much more detailed and students seem more invested in their learning as they are able to track it and see progress on very specific objectives along the way. In the past, I had always thought of objectives as more for the teacher than for the student, but this process has made me see the importance of each student understanding each objective within a unit. When students could understand and track their progress towards mastering each objective, they wanted to improve! More so, they were able to see how all of their work from the unit was connected and scaffolded which made lessons much more engaging as they saw a purpose to each day."*

The following page has an example of a lesson that was designed using a deconstructed standard and the Objective Builder. As you review the lesson, notice how it embodies the elements of TCD.

Date	Conceptual Understanding	Authors and illustrators have different roles in telling a story.			
Getting Ready to Learn	Focus Standard & Focus Dimension(s)	RL.K.6. With prompting and support, name the author and illustrator of a story, and define the role of each in telling the story. Apply-Analyze-Factual-Conceptual-Procedural-Metacognitive			
	Supporting Standard(s)	SL.K.6. Speak audibly and express thoughts, feelings and ideas clearly.			
	Objective	Students will **find coherence** between the role of an author and an illustrator using XX story to map their relationships on Voice Thread.			
	Flexible Grouping:	Group 'A' will work in a small group the paraprofessional so they can receive additional support with accessing the text. The parent volunteers will assist with getting students on to Voice Thread.			
			Accommodations		
			Alternative Means of Representation http://www.udlcenter.org/aboutudl/udlguidelines/principle1	Alternative Means of Action and Expression http://www.udlcenter.org/aboutudl/udlguidelines/principle2	Alternative Means of Engagement http://www.udlcenter.org/aboutudl/udlguidelines/principle3
	Activator/Motivator	Provide students with copy of book cover. The terms will be circled and have an arrow pointing to the box where students will trace/write (depending on level) the term. Explain each word and how the pictures relate. Have students repeat then write/trace word. Ask students to say again what the author and illustrator does in a story.	2.1 Clarify additional vocabulary for students needing more support	6.2 Provide a visual checklist	N/A
Acquire and Integrate Knowledge OR Extend and Refine Knowledge OR Meaningful Use	Learning Activities (Use teaching model that matches learning target) • **Connect to content** • **Connect to practitioner** • **Connect across disciplines** • **Connect to self**	• Teacher reads story aloud, shows pictures and asks text-dependent questions about the connection between the words and the pictures • Break students into small groups with assigned adult • Students are provided a copy of a story that can be marked • Students read (or are read to depending on level) while pointing at words • Students are asked to find the similarities between what was read and the picture • Students highlight/color words and image features in the same color that are related • As students complete, they go to the Voice Thread station to record their responses with their names • Early finishers, advance to another story to make connections	2.5. Make explicit links between text and illustrations	5.1 Use multi media for communication 6.2 Embed coaches that model think-aloud	8.3 Create cooperative learning groups
Closure	Review and Reflect on Learning	Whole class review: Teacher asks students who wants to share their work. Teacher asks, how do the author and the illustrator help each other throughout a story?	3.4 Allow for review	N/A	9.3 Develop reflection
	Assess Learning	Teacher will document students' understanding listening to their short recordings on Voice Thread.	N/A	N/A	8.4 Provide timely feedback
Reinforce or Prepare for Learning	Home Extension • Memorizing • Accuracy and Speed • **Deepen Understanding** • Preparation	Deepen understanding by **match** the details of pictures with terms by selecting the terms from the word bank and writing on the line that points to an appropriate image on a book cover. (Tomorrow as a part of the activator, they will write the role of the author and illustrator and how they help each other in a story.)	N/A	6.2 Provide guides for completing HW.	8.4 Provide timely feedback

© 2011 Sheron Brown. Lesson Plan Framework

Date					
Getting Ready to Learn	**Conceptual Understanding**	Different characters can add to a story at different points in the story.			
	Focus Standard & Focus Dimension(s)	RL.1.6. Identify who is telling the story at various points in a text. Remember-Understand-Factual-Conceptual-Procedural-Metacognitive			
	Supporting Standard(s)	SL.1.6. Produce complete sentences when appropriate to task and situation.			
	Objective	Students will **explain** their process for identifying who is talking in a text by using their recording to write their explanation.			
	Flexible Grouping: Group 'A' will work in a small group with the co-teacher so they can receive additional support with accessing the text.				
			Accommodations		
			Alternative Means of Representation http://www.udlcenter.org/aboutudl/udlguidelines/principle1	Alternative Means of Action and Expression http://www.udlcenter.org/aboutudl/udlguidelines/principle2	Alternative Means of Engagement http://www.udlcenter.org/aboutudl/udlguidelines/principle3
	Activator/Motivator	Provide access to Wordia.com for students to engage in vocabulary activity. After 10 minutes ask students to share what they recall about the terms. Inform them that we will continue to use these terms throughout the week. Share and post visual definitions on the Word Wall and tell them to refer to the wall if they forget the meaning for today.	1.1 Allow different size dominoes for students who need to write in larger than average print	6.2 Provide a visual checklist	N/A
Acquire and Integrate Knowledge OR Extend and Refine Knowledge OR Meaningful Use	**Learning Activities** (Use teaching model that matches learning target) • **Connect to content** • **Connect to practitioner** • **Connect across disciplines** • **Connect to self**	• Before reading, teacher asks students to listen out for how many characters are in the part of the story they will read today • Teacher reads story aloud and asks text-dependent question at the end of each page • Ask students to write how many characters they think they heard in the story • Students re-read story to list each character's name in the story • Students marks where the speaker in the story changes • Students are asked to close their eyes and think about how they knew the speaker changed • Student digitally records what they did and thought to know when the speaker changed • Students listen to their recording to write their explanation of the process	1.3 Students are deliberately grouped with partners as competent interveners	6.2 Provide a visual checklist of the steps	7.1 Provide as much discretion and autonomy as possible 8.3 Create cooperative learning groups
Closure	**Review and Reflect on Learning**	Whole class review: Teacher shares his explanation and leads discussion on similarities with what students wrote.	3.4 Allow for review	N/A	9.3 Develop reflection
	Assess Learning	Teacher will document students' understanding by reading their written explanation.	N/A	N/A	8.4 Provide timely feedback
Reinforce or Prepare for Learning	**Home Extension** • **Memorizing** • **Accuracy and Speed** • **Deepen Understanding** • **Preparation**	Deepen understanding by **comparing** the details of the teacher's process and their process to highlight the similarities on both. (Copies will be made and stapled.) Then write 1-3 sentences to explain how both the teacher and student identified who was telling the story and different times in the text.	N/A	5.2 Allow students to submit HW electronically and/or recorded.	8.4 Provide timely feedback

© 2011 Sheron Brown. Lesson Plan Framework

Date					
Getting Ready to Learn	Conceptual Understanding	A character's point of view can be heard through their voice.			
	Focus Standard & Focus Dimension(s)	RL.2.6 Acknowledge difference in the points of view of characters, including speaking in a different voice for each character when reading dialogue. Remember-Understand-Factual-Conceptual-Procedural-Metacognitive			
	Supporting Standard(s)	SL.2.2. Recount or describe key ideas or details from a text read aloud or information presented orally or through other media.			
	Objective	Students will **identify** the differences in POV between the characters in XX book to generate a character chart that shows the different POV with a partner.			
	Flexible Grouping:	Group 'A' will work in a small group the co-teacher so they can receive additional support with accessing the text.			
			Accommodations		
			Alternative Means of Representation http://www.udlcenter.org/aboutudl/udlguidelines/principle1	Alternative Means of Action and Expression http://www.udlcenter.org/aboutudl/udlguidelines/principle2	Alternative Means of Engagement http://www.udlcenter.org/aboutudl/udlguidelines/principle3
	Activator/Motivator	Provide materials for students to begin making their vocabulary dominoes for the week. (They will exchange sets and play a game of dominoes during Lunch Friends on Friday.) After 10 minutes ask for the definition of Point of View (POV). Inform students there are ways to acknowledge POV and like detectives, we will figure out what those ways are over the next couple of days.	1.1 Allow different size dominoes for students who need to write in larger than average print	6.2 Provide a checklist	N/A
Acquire and Integrate Knowledge OR Extend and Refine Knowledge OR Meaningful Use	Learning Activities (Use teaching model that matches learning target) • Connect to content • Connect to practitioner • Connect across disciplines • Connect to self	• Teacher begins by reading aloud the beginning of the story using different voices for each character
• Teacher asks text-dependent questions to help students identify the way each character sees the situation
• Teachers provides character chart and students document responses as teacher models
• Students continue reading the story with partner and stops after each page to list the differences (groups are assigned different characters)
• Teacher distributes large chart paper
• Students answers on T chart: What is character X's POV? What is character Y's POV? How do you know
• Students share with whole class and ask each other questions | 1.3 Students are deliberately grouped with partners as competent interveners | 6.2 Provide a checklist of the steps | 7.1 Provide as much discretion and autonomy as possible

8.3 Create cooperative learning groups |
Closure	Review and Reflect on Learning	Whole class review: What were some ways you heard that helped us identify the POV of the different characters?	3.4 Allow for review	N/A	9.3 Develop reflection
	Assess Learning	Teacher will document students' understanding as they present to the class.	N/A	N/A	8.4 Provide timely feedback
Reinforce or Prepare for Learning	Home Extension • Memorizing • Accuracy and Speed • **Deepen Understanding** • Preparation	Deepen understanding by **explaining** the process of how they were able to recognize (acknowledge) the POV of the characters they focused. (Tomorrow they will identify differences in characters POV without teacher prompting, so they will use their process.)	N/A	5.2 Allow students to submit HW electronically and/or recorded.	8.4 Provide timely feedback

© 2011 Sheron Brown, Lesson Plan Framework

Date	Conceptual Understanding	My point of view could make the telling of a story different than the narrator or character.			
Getting Ready to Learn	Focus Standard & Focus Dimension(s)	RL.3.6 Distinguish their own point of view from that of the narrator or those of the characters. Remember-Understand-Factual-Conceptual-Procedural-Metacognitive			
	Supporting Standard(s)	W.3.6. With guidance and support from adults, use technology to produce and publish writing using keyboarding skills as well as to interact and collaborate with others.			
	Objective	Students will **identify** the steps used to distinguish using (a short narrative) to generate an explanation in list format on their triad team's wiki page.			
	Flexible Grouping: Group 'A' will work in a small group the co-teacher so they can receive additional support with accessing the text.				
			Accommodations		
			Alternative Means of Representation http://www.udlcenter.org/aboutudl/udlguidelines/principle1	Alternative Means of Action and Expression http://www.udlcenter.org/aboutudl/udlguidelines/principle2	Alternative Means of Engagement http://www.udlcenter.org/aboutudl/udlguidelines/principle3
	Activator/Motivator	Provide materials for students to begin making their vocabulary dominoes for the week. (They will exchange sets and play a game of dominoes during Lunch Friends on Friday.) After 10 minutes ask for the definition of distinguish. Inform students there are steps for distinguishing and they will figure out the steps. Also let them know that first they are learning how to distinguish well because later in the week they will distinguish between their own POV and the character in the class text.	1.1 Allow different size dominoes for students who need to write in larger than average print	6.2 Provide a checklist	N/A
Acquire and Integrate Knowledge OR Extend and Refine Knowledge OR Meaningful Use	Learning Activities (Use teaching model that matches learning target) • Connect to content • Connect to practitioner • Connect across disciplines • Connect to self	Have students close read a short text in their triads to distinguish 3 characters POV: • Read once quietly • Read 2nd time paragraph at a time with team • After each paragraph discuss which character says/believes/feels which way • Write notes in their "writer's log" • Continue for each paragraph • Discuss what the author did to help distinguish how each character spoke/believed/felt • Discuss other ways they were able to distinguish these differences • Generate an agreed upon list and post to their team wiki titled "How to Distinguish POV"	1.3 Students are deliberately grouped with partners as competent interveners	6.2 Provide a checklist of the steps	7.1 Provide as much discretion and autonomy as possible 8.3 Create cooperative learning groups
Closure	Review and Reflect on Learning	Whole class review: What were some ways the author helped you distinguish the POV of the characters? How did those ways help you distinguish POV?	3.4 Allow for review	N/A	9.3 Develop reflection
	Assess Learning	Review the team wikis and insert notes. They will review their feedback notes tomorrow.	N/A	N/A	8.4 Provide timely feedback
Reinforce or Prepare for Learning	Home Extension • Memorizing • Accuracy and Speed • Deepen Understanding • Preparation	Prepare for tomorrow's assignment by **contrasting** the details of a time when their POV differed from a friend or family and explain at what actions show the differences.	N/A	5.2 Allow students to submit HW electronically	8.4 Provide timely feedback

© 2011 Sheron Brown. Lesson Plan Framework

Date	Conceptual Understanding	Third person narrators may have a limited point of view in comparison to first-person narrators.		
Getting Ready to Learn	Focus Standard & Focus Dimension(s)	RL.4.6 Compare and contrast the point of view from which different stories are narrated, including the difference between first- and third-person narrations. Remember-Understand-Factual-Conceptual-Procedural-Metacognitive		
	Supporting Standard(s)	SL.4.1. Engage effectively in a range of collaborative discussions with diverse partners on *grade 4 topics and texts*, building on others' ideas and expressing their own clearly. L.4.4. Determine or clarify the meaning of unknown and multiple-meaning words and phrases based on *grade 4 reading and content* choosing flexibly from a range of strategies.		
	Objective	Students will **classify** the attributes of first and third person narration using 2 versions of a single story to generate a compare/contrast chart with a partner.		
	Flexible Grouping: David, Kanisha, Anita and Deshawn are struggling readers. I will sit with them in a small group to support their reading of the text and facilitate a student led discussion to classify the attributes.				

			Accommodations	
		Alternative Means of Representation http://www.udlcenter.org/aboutudl/udlguidelines/principle1	Alternative Means of Action and Expression http://www.udlcenter.org/aboutudl/udlguidelines/principle2	Alternative Means of Engagement http://www.udlcenter.org/aboutudl/udlguidelines/principle3
	Activator/Motivator	N/A	6.2 Embed "stop and think prompts"	N/A
Acquire and Integrate Knowledge OR Extend and Refine Knowledge OR Meaningful Use	Learning Activities (Use teaching model that matches learning target) • Connect to content • Connect to practitioner • Connect across disciplines • Connect to self	Provide three images each with the appropriate label they represent: first-, second- and third-person. Ask students to examine the images and write one sentence under each that **exemplifies** the differences between the terms. After allowing a few students to share their activator responses, confirm/correct the meaning of each term. Inform students that they will focus on only 1st and 3rd person for the unit. Briefly share why will not focus on 2nd. Explain that they will work with their partner to read two stories, one written in each person, to list and classify the similarities and differences in how the stories are told. Post the directions and check to ensure their understanding of the terms (first- and third- person) and the posted directions. Allow partners to rotate to three other partnerships to share their classifications and note similarities. They may modify their attributes at this time if they choose.	3.1 Activate prior knowledge 3.4 Embed new ideas in familiar ideas and context	5.2 Allow students the choice of using Inspiration software 6.4 Show representation of progress	7.1 Provide as much discretion and autonomy as possible 8.3 Create cooperative learning groups
Closure	Review and Reflect on Learning	Whole class review: What were the similarities in attributes you gathered when sharing with the other partners?	3.4 Allow for review	N/A	9.3 Develop reflection
	Assess Learning	Collect their charts to determine their level of understanding.	N/A	N/A	8.4 Provide timely feedback
Reinforce or Prepare for Learning	Home Extension • Memorizing • Accuracy and Speed • Deepen Understanding • Preparation	Prepare for tomorrow's assignment by **recalling** and **explaining** the steps you used to *compare and contrast*	N/A	5.2 Allow students to submit HW electronically	8.4 Provide timely feedback

© 2011 Sheron Brown. Lesson Plan Framework

			Accommodations		
			Alternative Means of Representation http://www.udlcenter.org/aboutudl/udlguidelines/principle1	Alternative Means of Action and Expression http://www.udlcenter.org/aboutudl/udlguidelines/principle2	Alternative Means of Engagement http://www.udlcenter.org/aboutudl/udlguidelines/principle3
Date	Conceptual Understanding	An individual's point of view influences how they depict a written or spoken account.			
Getting Ready to Learn	Focus Standard & Focus Dimension(s)	RL.5.6 Describe how a narrator or speaker's point of view influences how events are described. Remember-Understand-Procedural-Metacognitive			
	Supporting Standard(s)	SL.5.1 Engage effectively in a range of collaborative discussions with diverse partners on grade 5 topics and texts, building on others' ideas and expressing their own clearly			
	Objective	Students will **construct** a model that shows the structure of a *description* using bookrags.com to present the components of a descriptive essay to their peers.			
	Flexible Grouping: Carlos, Denia, Sandra and Ricky are 1 day ahead of the class. They will work in a small group on the following: **paraphrase** the meaning of specific terminology: *narrator, speaker, point of view, influence, event, describe* using the method of their choice to verbally confirm their understanding in their group. (Remember-Understand-Factual) They will also **explain** how assumptions *influence point of view* by using an author's bio and his written account to depict the connections between the two in their group. (Remember-Understand-Conceptual)				
	Activator/Motivator	1-Pose a question; 2-Allow students to share brainstormed responses; 3-Capture responses on the board: How are descriptions structured?	N/A	6.2 Embed "stop and think prompts"	N/A
Acquire and Integrate Knowledge OR Extend and Refine Knowledge OR Meaningful Use	Learning Activities (Use teaching model that matches learning target) • Connect to content • Connect to practitioner • Connect across disciplines • Connect to self	Inform students that descriptions or descriptive essays are different than narratives and that we need to be clear about the difference because they will write a descriptive essay in the days to come. Briefly share how a narrative is structured, then inform the students they will spend the remainder of the period determining how a descriptive essay is structured. 1. Read the descriptive essay once. Read it a second time and list specific components that you notice. Discuss your list with your partner. Revise if you feel it is necessary. 2. Construct a visual model that best helps you understand the structure of a descriptive essay. 3. Read the bookrags.com article: *How to Write a Descriptive Essay*. Based on the components explained, revise your model. 4. Share your revised model in quads, and revise once more if you feel it is necessary.	3.1 Activate prior knowledge 3.4 Embed new ideas in familiar ideas and context	5.2 Allow students the choice of using Inspiration software 6.3 Provide checklist and guide for note taking 6.4 Show representation of progress	7.1 Provide as much discretion and autonomy as possible 8.3 Create cooperative learning groups
Closure	Review and Reflect on Learning	Whole class review: How did your model change after reading about the components?	3.4 Allow for review	N/A	9.3 Develop reflection
	Assess Learning	Collect their models to determine their level of understanding.	N/A	N/A	8.4 Provide timely feedback
Reinforce or Prepare for Learning	Home Extension • Memorizing • Accuracy and Speed • Deepen understanding • Preparation	Prepare for tomorrow's assignment by **paraphrasing** the meaning of specific terminology: *narrator, speaker, point of view, influence, event, describe*	N/A	5.2 Allow students to submit HW electronically	8.4 Provide timely feedback

© 2011 Sheron Brown. Lesson Plan Framework

TCD Practice: Use a deconstructed standard to design a lesson for **acquisition or initial learning** *with this modified lesson design framework.*

Conceptual Understanding	
Focus Standard	
Supporting Standard	
Objective	
Flexible Grouping	

		UDL ACCOMODATIONS
Activator/ Motivator		*Alternatives Means of Expression*
Learning Activities (Use teaching model that matches learning target) • Connect to content • Connect to practitioner • Connect across disciplines • Connect to self		*Alternative Means of Representation* *Alternative Means of Expression* *Alternative Means of Engagement*
Review and Reflect on Learning		*Alternative Means of Representation* *Alternative Means of Engagement*
Assess Learning		*Alternative Means of Engagement*

Home Extension • Memorizing • Accuracy and Speed • Deepen understanding • Preparation		*Alternative Means of Expression*

*TCD Practice: Use a deconstructed standard to design a lesson for **extended learning and practice** with this modified lesson design framework.*

Conceptual Understanding		
Focus Standard		
Supporting Standard		
Objective		
Flexible Grouping		
		UDL ACCOMODATIONS
Activator/ Motivator		*Alternatives Means of Expression*
Learning Activities (Use teaching model that matches learning target) • **Connect to content** • **Connect to practitioner** • **Connect across disciplines** • **Connect to self**		*Alternative Means of Representation* *Alternative Means of Expression* *Alternative Means of Engagement*
Review and Reflect on Learning		*Alternative Means of Representation* *Alternative Means of Engagement*
Assess Learning		*Alternative Means of Engagement*
Home Extension • **Memorizing** • **Accuracy and Speed** • **Deepen understanding** • **Preparation**		*Alternative Means of Expression*

*TCD Practice: Use a deconstructed standard to design a lesson for **relevant and meaningful learning** with this modified lesson design framework.*

Conceptual Understanding	
Focus Standard	
Supporting Standard	
Objective	
Flexible Grouping	

		UDL ACCOMODATIONS
Activator/ Motivator		*Alternatives Means of Expression*
Learning Activities (Use teaching model that matches learning target) • **Connect to content** • **Connect to practitioner** • **Connect across disciplines** • **Connect to self**		*Alternative Means of Representation* *Alternative Means of Expression* *Alternative Means of Engagement*
Review and Reflect on Learning		*Alternative Means of Representation* *Alternative Means of Engagement*
Assess Learning		*Alternative Means of Engagement*

Home Extension • **Memorizing** • **Accuracy and Speed** • **Deepen understanding** • **Preparation**		*Alternative Means of Expression*

Back to Grounding.

In a nutshell, one purpose of the CCSS is to encourage **teaching** that fosters **disciplinary thinking** and **knowledge** production. Several excerpts from the CCSS documents point to this assertion. Two excerpts follow:

"**Students** *who are college and career ready in reading, writing, speaking, listening and language...demonstrate independence...build strong* **content knowledge**...*respond to the* **varying demands** *of audience, task, purpose and* **discipline**...**comprehend** *as well as* **critique**...**value evidence**...*use technology and capably...come to understand other* **perspectives** *and* **cultures**" *(p. 7).*

"*To become college and career ready, students must grapple with works of exceptional craft and thought whose range extends across genres, cultures, and centuries. Such works offer profound insights into the human condition and serve as models for students' own thinking and writing. Along with high quality contemporary works, these texts should be chosen from among seminal U.S. documents, the classics of American literature, and the timeless dramas of Shakespeare. Through wide and deep reading of literature and literary nonfiction of steadily increasing sophistication, students gain a reservoir of literary and cultural knowledge, references, and images; the ability to evaluate intricate arguments; and the capacity to surmount the challenges posed by complex texts*" *(p. 35).*

Take another look at the second quote...

"To become college and career ready, **students must** grapple with works of **exceptional craft and thought** whose range **extends across genres, cultures, and centuries.** Such works... profound **insights**... condition and serve as **models** for **students' own thinking** and writing. Along with high-quality contemporary works, these texts should be chosen from among **seminal** U.S. documents, the classics of American literature, and the timeless dramas of Shakespeare. Through wide and deep reading literature and literary nonfiction of **steadily increasing sophistication,** students gain a reservoir of **literary and cultural knowledge,** references, and images; the ability to **evaluate** intricate arguments; and the **capacity** to surmount the challenges posed by complex texts" (p. 35).

Annotations: Conceptual Understanding, Teaching, Discipline Domains, Cognitive Process, Knowledge Dimension

There are many other statements in the standards documents that point to the claim. A close read of the document will reveal evidence repeatedly.

Who Said So?

Hundreds of research studies and thousands of books outline how to teach so that students generate new knowledge as you foster disciplinary thinking. The TCD process distills multiple theories by synthesizing the essential elements of their connecting ideas to make what appears overwhelming, readily applicable.

The table below displays the synthesis.

TEACH so that students THINK and generate KNOWLEDGE
Embedded in the Standards

Table III. The 3 Dimensions of TCD

Teach	Think	Knowledge
• CONTRIBUTIONS: Dimensions of Learning; Classroom Instruction that Works; The Art and Science of Teaching; Visible Learning (these works represent hundreds more)	• CONTRIBUTIONS: Making Thinking Visible; Taxonomy for Learning, Teaching, and Assessing; Concept-Based Curriculum and Instruction for the Thinking Classroom (these works represent hundreds more)	• CONTRIBUTIONS: The Schoolwide Enrichment Model; Using the Parallel Curriculum Model in Urban Settings; The Parallel Curriculum (these works represent hundreds more)
• APPLICATION: The purpose of the lesson dictates the teaching model. For example, when teaching for understanding, models that foster acquisition and integration of knowledge should be considered. The TCD structure visually highlights the lesson's purpose.	• APPLICATION: Students must think so they can learn. The choice the thinking demands must be deliberate. The content and major ideas of the discipline being studied must be also be considered deliberately. The TCD objective stems focus on thinking within the concepts of the discipline.	• APPLICATION: Deliberate choices about disciplinary thinking support the development of knowledge as students move from being novice level learners toward expert level learners. The TCD's structure and objective stems integrate disciplinary thinking, content and the advancement of the learner.
• RELEVANCE: The teaching model must support the level of thinking required.	• RELEVANCE: The level of thinking must support the development of knowledge desired.	• RELEVANCE: The consideration of building knowledge in the discipline supports the quest for rigor in instruction.

Notes to Remember

1. The conceptual understanding is in the standard.
2. Deconstructing the standard allow you to identify supporting standards.
3. Objective stems are the beginning of creating clear learning targets.
4. Create differentiated groups using objective stems.
5. Objective stems provide guidance for lesson design.
6. Tiered objective stems allow for homework with purpose.
7. Assessment is built in and therefore aligned with the lesson.

List your additional closing notes.

About the Author

Sheron Brown, PhD, is the Chief Performance Strategist at EdSolutions by Design. At EdSolutions, Dr. Brown partners with school leaders to facilitate the creation of school excellence plans and organizational learning plans. Dr. Brown also designs tools that help good educators become great educators. Dr. Brown is a passionate change agent and systems-thinker who supports leaders in achieving excellence through the development of their people and through continuous improvement. She has served as a classroom teacher, building-level leader, district leader, professional developer, instructional coach, leadership coach, adjunct professor, and a Baldrige Examiner. You can find her on www.sheronbrownphd.com or connect with her on www.linkedin.com/in/sheronbrownphd.

Send your thoughts, comments, feedback or testimonials. We want to improve. We want to hear from you!

Connect with Dr. B. through...

About.me: About.me: http://about.me/sheronbrownphd
Sheronbrownphd Blog Micro-PD for Leadership and Instructional Resources: http://sheronbrownphd.com/
LinkedIn for Micro-PD on the Common Core and Leadership: www.linkedin.com/in/sheronbrownphd/
Twitter for Micro-PD on the Common Core and Leadership: http://twitter.com/DrSBrown
Pinterest for Common Core and Instructional Resources: http://pinterest.com/drsbrown/

For the resources in the practice journal, visit www.sheronbrownphd.com.

References

Anderson, L.W., Krathwaohl, D. R., Airasian, P. W., Cruikshank, K. A., Mayer, R. E., Pintrich, P. R., Raths, J. & Wittrock, M.C. (2001). *A taxonomy for learning, teaching, and assessing: A revision of Bloom's taxonomy of educational objectives* (Abridged ed.). New York: Longman.

Brown, S. M. (2012, October 15). Warning: Poor lesson plans means students learn poorly [Blog post]. Retrieved from http://sheronbrownphd.com/2012/10/15/warning-poor-lesson-plans-mean-students-learn-poorly/

Common Core State Standards Initiative. (2010, June). *Preparing America's students for college & career*. Retrieved from http://www.corestandards.org

Dean, C. B., Hubbell, E. R., Pitler, H. & Stone, B. (2012). *Classroom instruction that works: Research-based strategies for increasing student achievement*. (2nd ed.). Alexandria, VA: ASCD.

Erickson, H. L. (2007). *Concept-based curriculum and instruction for the thinking classroom*. Thousand Oaks, CA: Corwin Press.

Hattie, J. (2009). *Visible learning: A synthesis of over 800 meta-analysis relating to achievement*. New York: Routledge.

Kaplan, S. N., Guzman, I., & Tomlinson, C. A. (2009). *Using the parallel curriculum model in urban settings: Grades k-8*. Thousand Oaks, CA: Corwin Press.

PARCC Proposal. (2012, August). *PARCC college-ready determination policy in English and mathematics & policy and general content claims for PARCC performance levels*. Retrieved from http://www.parcconline.org/sites/parcc/files/PARCCDraftCRDPolicyandPolicyandGeneralContentClaimsforPLDs7_12_12.pdf

Hedrick, K., & Flannagan, J.S. (2009). Ascending intellectual demand in the parallel curriculum model. In C. A. Tomlinson, S. N. Kaplan, J. S. Renzulli, J. H. Purcell, J. H. Leppien, D. E. Burns, C.A. Strickland &, M. B. Imbeau (2nd ed.). *The parallel curriculum: A design to develop learner potential and challenge advanced learners* (pp. 233-293). Thousand Oaks, CA: Corwin Press.

Marzano, R. J. (2007). *The art and science of teaching: A comprehensive framework for effective instruction*. Alexandria, VA: ASCD.

Marzano, R. J., Pinkering, D. J., Arredondo, D. E., Blackburn, G. J., Brandt, R. S., Moffet, C. A., Paynter, D. E., Pollock, J. E., & Whisler, J. S. (1997). *Dimensions of learning*. (2nd ed.) Alexandria, VA: ASCD.

Renzulli, J. S. & Reis, S. M. (1997). *The schoolwide enrichment model; A how-to guide for educational excellence*. (2nd ed.). Mansfield Center, CT: Creative Learning Press.

Ritchhart, R., Church, M. & Morrison, K. (2011). *Making thinking visible: How to promote engagement, understanding, and independence for all learners*. San Francisco, CA: Jossey-Bass.

Smarter Balanced Assessment Consortium. (2013, April). *Initial Achievement Level Descriptors and College Content-Readiness policy.* Retrieved from http://www.smarterbalanced.org/wordpress/wp-content/uploads/2012/11/Smarter-Balanced-ELA-Literacy-ALDs.pdf

Credits

Images Courtesy of:
adamr "Tablet Computer and Book"
aopsan "Empty Blackboard With Wooden Frame"
jannoon028 "Business Hand Holding Show"
Keerati "Opened Laptop"
Mr. Lightman "Brain Design By Cogs and Gears"
Ohmega1982 "Social Networking Concept"
Scottchan "Wooden Sign," "Achievement Road Sign," "Blackboard with Chalks"
Stuart Miles "Pointing Future on Blackboard, Opportunity Definition Button,
at FreeDigitalPhotos.net

Appendices

Appendix A

    Common Core State Standards for Reading Literature

Appendix B

    Common Core State Standards for Reading Informational Texts

Appendix C

    Common Core State Standards for Writing

Appendix D

    Common Core State Standards for Speaking and Listening

Appendix E

    Common Core State Standards for Language

Appendix A: Common Core State Standards for Reading Literature

Kindergarten
Key Ideas and Details
CCSS.ELA-Literacy.RL.K.1 With prompting and support, ask and answer questions about key details in a text.
CCSS.ELA-Literacy.RL.K.2 With prompting and support, retell familiar stories, including key details.
CCSS.ELA-Literacy.RL.K.3 With prompting and support, identify characters, settings, and major events in a story.
Craft and Structure
CCSS.ELA-Literacy.RL.K.4 Ask and answer questions about unknown words in a text.
CCSS.ELA-Literacy.RL.K.5 Recognize common types of texts (e.g., storybooks, poems).
CCSS.ELA-Literacy.RL.K.6 With prompting and support, name the author and illustrator of a story and define the role of each in telling the story.
Integration of Knowledge and Ideas
CCSS.ELA-Literacy.RL.K.7 With prompting and support, describe the relationship between illustrations and the story in which they appear (e.g., what moment in a story an illustration depicts).
(RL.K.8 not applicable to literature)
CCSS.ELA-Literacy.RL.K.9 With prompting and support, compare and contrast the adventures and experiences of characters in familiar stories.
Range of Reading and Level of Text Complexity
CCSS.ELA-Literacy.RL.K.10 Actively engage in group reading activities with purpose and understanding.

First Grade
Key Ideas and Details
CCSS.ELA-Literacy.RL.1.1 Ask and answer questions about key details in a text.
CCSS.ELA-Literacy.RL.1.2 Retell stories, including key details, and demonstrate understanding of their central message or lesson.
CCSS.ELA-Literacy.RL.1.3 Describe characters, settings, and major events in a story, using key details.
Craft and Structure
CCSS.ELA-Literacy.RL.1.4 Identify words and phrases in stories or poems that suggest feelings or appeal to the senses.
CCSS.ELA-Literacy.RL.1.5 Explain major differences between books that tell stories and books that give information, drawing on a wide reading of a range of text types.
CCSS.ELA-Literacy.RL.1.6 Identify who is telling the story at various points in a text.
Integration of Knowledge and Ideas
CCSS.ELA-Literacy.RL.1.7 Use illustrations and details in a story to describe its characters, setting, or events.
(RL.1.8 not applicable to literature)
CCSS.ELA-Literacy.RL.1.9 Compare and contrast the adventures and experiences of characters in stories.
Range of Reading and Level of Text Complexity
CCSS.ELA-Literacy.RL.1.10 With prompting and support, read prose and poetry of appropriate complexity for grade 1.

Second Grade
Key Ideas and Details
CCSS.ELA-Literacy.RL.2.1 Ask and answer such questions as *who, what, where, when, why*, and *how* to demonstrate understanding of key details in a text.
CCSS.ELA-Literacy.RL.2.2 Recount stories, including fables and folktales from diverse cultures, and determine their central message, lesson, or moral.
CCSS.ELA-Literacy.RL.2.3 Describe how characters in a story respond to major events and challenges.
Craft and Structure
CCSS.ELA-Literacy.RL.2.4 Describe how words and phrases (e.g., regular beats, alliteration, rhymes, repeated lines) supply rhythm and meaning in a story, poem, or song.
CCSS.ELA-Literacy.RL.2.5 Describe the overall structure of a story, including describing how the beginning introduces the story and the ending concludes the action.
CCSS.ELA-Literacy.RL.2.6 Acknowledge differences in the points of view of characters, including by speaking

in a different voice for each character when reading dialogue aloud.
Integration of Knowledge and Ideas
CCSS.ELA-Literacy.RL.2.7 Use information gained from the illustrations and words in a print or digital text to demonstrate understanding of its characters, setting, or plot.
(RL.2.8 not applicable to literature)
CCSS.ELA-Literacy.RL.2.9 Compare and contrast two or more versions of the same story (e.g., Cinderella stories) by different authors or from different cultures.
Range of Reading and Level of Text Complexity
CCSS.ELA-Literacy.RL.2.10 By the end of the year, read and comprehend literature, including stories and poetry, in the grades 2–3 text complexity band proficiently, with scaffolding as needed at the high end of the range.

Third Grade
Key Ideas and Details
CCSS.ELA-Literacy.RL.3.1 Ask and answer questions to demonstrate understanding of a text, referring explicitly to the text as the basis for the answers.
CCSS.ELA-Literacy.RL.3.2 Recount stories, including fables, folktales, and myths from diverse cultures; determine the central message, lesson, or moral and explain how it is conveyed through key details in the text.
CCSS.ELA-Literacy.RL.3.3 Describe characters in a story (e.g., their traits, motivations, or feelings) and explain how their actions contribute to the sequence of events
Craft and Structure
CCSS.ELA-Literacy.RL.3.4 Determine the meaning of words and phrases as they are used in a text, distinguishing literal from nonliteral language.
CCSS.ELA-Literacy.RL.3.5 Refer to parts of stories, dramas, and poems when writing or speaking about a text, using terms such as chapter, scene, and stanza; describe how each successive part builds on earlier sections.
CCSS.ELA-Literacy.RL.3.6 Distinguish their own point of view from that of the narrator or those of the characters.
Integration of Knowledge and Ideas
CCSS.ELA-Literacy.RL.3.7 Explain how specific aspects of a text's illustrations contribute to what is conveyed by the words in a story (e.g., create mood, emphasize aspects of a character or setting)
(RL.3.8 not applicable to literature)
CCSS.ELA-Literacy.RL.3.9 Compare and contrast the themes, settings, and plots of stories written by the same author about the same or similar characters (e.g., in books from a series)
Range of Reading and Level of Text Complexity
CCSS.ELA-Literacy.RL.3.10 By the end of the year, read and comprehend literature, including stories, dramas, and poetry, at the high end of the grades 2–3 text complexity band independently and proficiently.

Fourth Grade
Key Ideas and Details
CCSS.ELA-Literacy.RL.4.1 Refer to details and examples in a text when explaining what the text says explicitly and when drawing inferences from the text.
CCSS.ELA-Literacy.RL.4.2 Determine a theme of a story, drama, or poem from details in the text; summarize the text.
CCSS.ELA-Literacy.RL.4.3 Describe in depth a character, setting, or event in a story or drama, drawing on specific details in the text (e.g., a character's thoughts, words, or actions).
Craft and Structure
CCSS.ELA-Literacy.RL.4.4 Determine the meaning of words and phrases as they are used in a text, including those that allude to significant characters found in mythology (e.g., Herculean).
CCSS.ELA-Literacy.RL.4.5 Explain major differences between poems, drama, and prose, and refer to the structural elements of poems (e.g., verse, rhythm, meter) and drama (e.g., casts of characters, settings, descriptions, dialogue, stage directions) when writing or speaking about a text.
CCSS.ELA-Literacy.RL.4.6 Compare and contrast the point of view from which different stories are narrated, including the difference between first- and third-person narrations.
Integration of Knowledge and Ideas

CCSS.ELA-Literacy.RL.4.7 Make connections between the text of a story or drama and a visual or oral presentation of the text, identifying where each version reflects specific descriptions and directions in the text.
(RL.4.8 not applicable to literature)
CCSS.ELA-Literacy.RL.4.9 Compare and contrast the treatment of similar themes and topics (e.g., opposition of good and evil) and patterns of events (e.g., the quest) in stories, myths, and traditional literature from different cultures.
Range of Reading and Level of Text Complexity
CCSS.ELA-Literacy.RL.4.10 By the end of the year, read and comprehend literature, including stories, dramas, and poetry, in the grades 4–5 text complexity band proficiently, with scaffolding as needed at the high end of the range.

Fifth Grade
Key Ideas and Details
CCSS.ELA-Literacy.RL.5.1 Quote accurately from a text when explaining what the text says explicitly and when drawing inferences from the text.
CCSS.ELA-Literacy.RL.5.2 Determine a theme of a story, drama, or poem from details in the text, including how characters in a story or drama respond to challenges or how the speaker in a poem reflects upon a topic; summarize the text.
CCSS.ELA-Literacy.RL.5.3 Compare and contrast two or more characters, settings, or events in a story or drama, drawing on specific details in the text (e.g., how characters interact).
Craft and Structure
CCSS.ELA-Literacy.RL.5.4 Determine the meaning of words and phrases as they are used in a text, including figurative language such as metaphors and similes.
CCSS.ELA-Literacy.RL.5.5 Explain how a series of chapters, scenes, or stanzas fits together to provide the overall structure of a particular story, drama, or poem.
CCSS.ELA-Literacy.RL.5.6 Describe how a narrator's or speaker's point of view influences how events are described.
Integration of Knowledge and Ideas
CCSS.ELA-Literacy.RL.5.7 Analyze how visual and multimedia elements contribute to the meaning, tone, or beauty of a text (e.g., graphic novel, multimedia presentation of fiction, folktale, myth, poem).
(RL.5.8 not applicable to literature)
CCSS.ELA-Literacy.RL.5.9 Compare and contrast stories in the same genre (e.g., mysteries and adventure stories) on their approaches to similar themes and topics.
Range of Reading and Level of Text Complexity
CCSS.ELA-Literacy.RL.5.10 By the end of the year, read and comprehend literature, including stories, dramas, and poetry, at the high end of the grades 4–5 text complexity band independently and proficiently.

to or viewing an audio, video, or live version of the text, including contrasting what they "see" and "hear" when reading the text to what they perceive when they listen or watch.
(RL.6.8 not applicable to literature)
CCSS.ELA-Literacy.RL.6.9 Compare and contrast texts in different forms or genres (e.g., stories and poems; historical novels and fantasy stories) in terms of their approaches to similar themes and topics.
Range of Reading and Level of Text Complexity
CCSS.ELA-Literacy.RL.6.10 By the end of the year, read and comprehend literature, including stories, dramas, and poems, in the grades 6–8 text complexity band proficiently, with scaffolding as needed at the high end of the range.

Appendix B: Common Core State Standards for Reading Informational Texts

Kindergarten
Key Ideas and Details
CCSS.ELA-Literacy.RI.K.1 With prompting and support, ask and answer questions about key details in a text.
CCSS.ELA-Literacy.RI.K.2 With prompting and support, identify the main topic and retell key details of a text.
CCSS.ELA-Literacy.RI.K.3 With prompting and support, describe the connection between two individuals, events, ideas, or pieces of information in a text.
Craft and Structure
CCSS.ELA-Literacy.RI.K.4 With prompting and support, ask and answer questions about unknown words in a text.
CCSS.ELA-Literacy.RI.K.5 Identify the front cover, back cover, and title page of a book.
CCSS.ELA-Literacy.RI.K.6 Name the author and illustrator of a text and define the role of each in presenting the ideas or information in a text.
Integration of Knowledge and Ideas
CCSS.ELA-Literacy.RI.K.7 With prompting and support, describe the relationship between illustrations and the text in which they appear (e.g., what person, place, thing, or idea in the text an illustration depicts).
CCSS.ELA-Literacy.RI.K.8 With prompting and support, identify the reasons an author gives to support points in a text.
CCSS.ELA-Literacy.RI.K.9 With prompting and support, identify basic similarities in and differences between two texts on the same topic (e.g., in illustrations, descriptions, or procedures).
Range of Reading and Level of Text Complexity
CCSS.ELA-Literacy.RI.K.10 Actively engage in group reading activities with purpose and understanding.

First Grade
Key Ideas and Details
CCSS.ELA-Literacy.RI.1.1 Ask and answer questions about key details in a text.
CCSS.ELA-Literacy.RI.1.2 Identify the main topic and retell key details of a text.
CCSS.ELA-Literacy.RI.1.3 Describe the connection between two individuals, events, ideas, or pieces of information in a text.
Craft and Structure
CCSS.ELA-Literacy.RI.1.4 Ask and answer questions to help determine or clarify the meaning of words and phrases in a text.
CCSS.ELA-Literacy.RI.1.5 Know and use various text features (e.g., headings, tables of contents, glossaries, electronic menus, icons) to locate key facts or information in a text.
CCSS.ELA-Literacy.RI.1.6 Distinguish between information provided by pictures or other illustrations and information provided by the words in a text.
Integration of Knowledge and Ideas
CCSS.ELA-Literacy.RI.1.7 Use the illustrations and details in a text to describe its key ideas.
CCSS.ELA-Literacy.RI.1.8 Identify the reasons an author gives to support points in a text.
CCSS.ELA-Literacy.RI.1.9 Identify basic similarities in and differences between two texts on the same topic (e.g., in illustrations, descriptions, or procedures).
Range of Reading and Level of Text Complexity
CCSS.ELA-Literacy.RI.1.10 With prompting and support, read informational texts appropriately complex for grade 1.

Second Grade
Key Ideas and Details
CCSS.ELA-Literacy.RI.2.1 Ask and answer such questions as *who*, *what*, *where*, *when*, *why*, and *how* to demonstrate understanding of key details in a text.
CCSS.ELA-Literacy.RI.2.2 Identify the main topic of a multiparagraph text as well as the focus of specific paragraphs within the text.
CCSS.ELA-Literacy.RI.2.3 Describe the connection between a series of historical events, scientific ideas or concepts, or steps in technical procedures in a text.

Craft and Structure
CCSS.ELA-Literacy.RI.2.4 Determine the meaning of words and phrases in a text relevant to a *grade 2 topic or subject area*.
CCSS.ELA-Literacy.RI.2.5 Know and use various text features (e.g., captions, bold print, subheadings, glossaries, indexes, electronic menus, icons) to locate key facts or information in a text efficiently.
CCSS.ELA-Literacy.RI.2.6 Identify the main purpose of a text, including what the author wants to answer, explain, or describe.
Integration of Knowledge and Ideas
CCSS.ELA-Literacy.RI.2.7 Explain how specific images (e.g., a diagram showing how a machine works) contribute to and clarify a text.
CCSS.ELA-Literacy.RI.2.8 Describe how reasons support specific points the author makes in a text.
CCSS.ELA-Literacy.RI.2.9 Compare and contrast the most important points presented by two texts on the same topic.
Range of Reading and Level of Text Complexity
CCSS.ELA-Literacy.RI.2.10 By the end of year, read and comprehend informational texts, including history/social studies, science, and technical texts, in the grades 2–3 text complexity band proficiently, with scaffolding as needed at the high end of the range.

Third Grade
Key Ideas and Details
CCSS.ELA-Literacy.RI.3.1 Ask and answer questions to demonstrate understanding of a text, referring explicitly to the text as the basis for the answers.
CCSS.ELA-Literacy.RI.3.2 Determine the main idea of a text; recount the key details and explain how they support the main idea.
CCSS.ELA-Literacy.RI.3.3 Describe the relationship between a series of historical events, scientific ideas or concepts, or steps in technical procedures in a text, using language that pertains to time, sequence, and cause/effect.
Craft and Structure
CCSS.ELA-Literacy.RI.3.4 Determine the meaning of general academic and domain-specific words and phrases in a text relevant to a *grade 3 topic or subject area*.
CCSS.ELA-Literacy.RI.3.5 Use text features and search tools (e.g., key words, sidebars, hyperlinks) to locate information relevant to a given topic efficiently.
CCSS.ELA-Literacy.RI.3.6 Distinguish their own point of view from that of the author of a text.
Integration of Knowledge and Ideas
CCSS.ELA-Literacy.RI.3.7 Use information gained from illustrations (e.g., maps, photographs) and the words in a text to demonstrate understanding of the text (e.g., where, when, why, and how key events occur).
CCSS.ELA-Literacy.RI.3.8 Describe the logical connection between particular sentences and paragraphs in a text (e.g., comparison, cause/effect, first/second/third in a sequence).
CCSS.ELA-Literacy.RI.3.9 Compare and contrast the most important points and key details presented in two texts on the same topic.
Range of Reading and Level of Text Complexity
CCSS.ELA-Literacy.RI.3.10 By the end of the year, read and comprehend informational texts, including history/social studies, science, and technical texts, at the high end of the grades 2–3 text complexity band independently and proficiently.

Fourth Grade
Key Ideas and Details
CCSS.ELA-Literacy.RI.4.1 Refer to details and examples in a text when explaining what the text says explicitly and when drawing inferences from the text.
CCSS.ELA-Literacy.RI.4.2 Determine the main idea of a text and explain how it is supported by key details; summarize the text.
CCSS.ELA-Literacy.RI.4.3 Explain events, procedures, ideas, or concepts in a historical, scientific, or technical text, including what happened and why, based on specific information in the text.
Craft and Structure

CCSS.ELA-Literacy.RI.4.4 Determine the meaning of general academic and domain-specific words or phrases in a text relevant to a *grade 4 topic or subject area*.
CCSS.ELA-Literacy.RI.4.5 Describe the overall structure (e.g., chronology, comparison, cause/effect, problem/solution) of events, ideas, concepts, or information in a text or part of a text.
CCSS.ELA-Literacy.RI.4.6 Compare and contrast a firsthand and secondhand account of the same event or topic; describe the differences in focus and the information provided.
Integration of Knowledge and Ideas
CCSS.ELA-Literacy.RI.4.7 Interpret information presented visually, orally, or quantitatively (e.g., in charts, graphs, diagrams, time lines, animations, or interactive elements on Web pages) and explain how the information contributes to an understanding of the text in which it appears.
CCSS.ELA-Literacy.RI.4.8 Explain how an author uses reasons and evidence to support particular points in a text.
CCSS.ELA-Literacy.RI.4.9 Integrate information from two texts on the same topic in order to write or speak about the subject knowledgeably.
Range of Reading and Level of Text Complexity
CCSS.ELA-Literacy.RI.4.10 By the end of year, read and comprehend informational texts, including history/social studies, science, and technical texts, in the grades 4–5 text complexity band proficiently, with scaffolding as needed at the high end of the range.

Fifth Grade
Key Ideas and Details
CCSS.ELA-Literacy.RI.5.1 Quote accurately from a text when explaining what the text says explicitly and when drawing inferences from the text.
CCSS.ELA-Literacy.RI.5.2 Determine two or more main ideas of a text and explain how they are supported by key details; summarize the text.
CCSS.ELA-Literacy.RI.5.3 Explain the relationships or interactions between two or more individuals, events, ideas, or concepts in a historical, scientific, or technical text based on specific information in the text.
Craft and Structure
CCSS.ELA-Literacy.RI.5.4 Determine the meaning of general academic and domain-specific words and phrases in a text relevant to a *grade 5 topic or subject area*.
CCSS.ELA-Literacy.RI.5.5 Compare and contrast the overall structure (e.g., chronology, comparison, cause/effect, problem/solution) of events, ideas, concepts, or information in two or more texts.
CCSS.ELA-Literacy.RI.5.6 Analyze multiple accounts of the same event or topic, noting important similarities and differences in the point of view they represent.
Integration of Knowledge and Ideas
CCSS.ELA-Literacy.RI.5.7 Draw on information from multiple print or digital sources, demonstrating the ability to locate an answer to a question quickly or to solve a problem efficiently.
CCSS.ELA-Literacy.RI.5.8 Explain how an author uses reasons and evidence to support particular points in a text, identifying which reasons and evidence support which point(s).
CCSS.ELA-Literacy.RI.5.9 Integrate information from several texts on the same topic in order to write or speak about the subject knowledgeably.
Range of Reading and Level of Text Complexity
CCSS.ELA-Literacy.RI.5.10 By the end of the year, read and comprehend informational texts, including history/social studies, science, and technical texts, at the high end of the grades 4–5 text complexity band independently and proficiently.

Appendix C: Common Core State Standards for Writing

Kindergarten
Text Types and Purposes
CCSS.ELA-Literacy.W.K.1 Use a combination of drawing, dictating, and writing to compose opinion pieces in which they tell a reader the topic or the name of the book they are writing about and state an opinion or preference about the topic or book (e.g., *My favorite book is...*).
CCSS.ELA-Literacy.W.K.2 Use a combination of drawing, dictating, and writing to compose informative/explanatory texts in which they name what they are writing about and supply some information about the topic.
CCSS.ELA-Literacy.W.K.3 Use a combination of drawing, dictating, and writing to narrate a single event or several loosely linked events, tell about the events in the order in which they occurred, and provide a reaction to what happened.
Production and Distribution of Writing
(W.K.4 begins in grade 3)
CCSS.ELA-Literacy.W.K.5 With guidance and support from adults, respond to questions and suggestions from peers and add details to strengthen writing as needed.
CCSS.ELA-Literacy.W.K.6 With guidance and support from adults, explore a variety of digital tools to produce and publish writing, including in collaboration with peers.
Research to Build and Present Knowledge
CCSS.ELA-Literacy.W.K.7 Participate in shared research and writing projects (e.g., explore a number of books by a favorite author and express opinions about them).
CCSS.ELA-Literacy.W.K.8 With guidance and support from adults, recall information from experiences or gather information from provided sources to answer a question.
(W.K.9 begins in grade 4)
Range of Writing
(W.K.10 begins in grade 3)

First Grade
Text Types and Purposes
CCSS.ELA-Literacy.W.1.1 Write opinion pieces in which they introduce the topic or name the book they are writing about, state an opinion, supply a reason for the opinion, and provide some sense of closure.
CCSS.ELA-Literacy.W.1.2 Write informative/explanatory texts in which they name a topic, supply some facts about the topic, and provide some sense of closure.
CCSS.ELA-Literacy.W.1.3 Write narratives in which they recount two or more appropriately sequenced events, include some details regarding what happened, use temporal words to signal event order, and provide some sense of closure.
Production and Distribution of Writing
(W.1.4 begins in grade 3)
CCSS.ELA-Literacy.W.1.5 With guidance and support from adults, focus on a topic, respond to questions and suggestions from peers, and add details to strengthen writing as needed.
CCSS.ELA-Literacy.W.1.6 With guidance and support from adults, use a variety of digital tools to produce and publish writing, including in collaboration with peers.
Research to Build and Present Knowledge
CCSS.ELA-Literacy.W.1.7 Participate in shared research and writing projects (e.g., explore a number of "how-to" books on a given topic and use them to write a sequence of instructions).
CCSS.ELA-Literacy.W.1.8 With guidance and support from adults, recall information from experiences or gather information from provided sources to answer a question.
(W.1.9 begins in grade 4)
Range of Writing
(W.1.10 begins in grade 3)

Second Grade
Text Types and Purposes

CCSS.ELA-Literacy.W.2.1 Write opinion pieces in which they introduce the topic or book they are writing about, state an opinion, supply reasons that support the opinion, use linking words (e.g., *because*, *and*, *also*) to connect opinion and reasons, and provide a concluding statement or section.
CCSS.ELA-Literacy.W.2.2 Write informative/explanatory texts in which they introduce a topic, use facts and definitions to develop points, and provide a concluding statement or section.
CCSS.ELA-Literacy.W.2.3 Write narratives in which they recount a well-elaborated event or short sequence of events, include details to describe actions, thoughts, and feelings, use temporal words to signal event order, and provide a sense of closure.
Production and Distribution of Writing
(W.2.4 begins in grade 3)
CCSS.ELA-Literacy.W.2.5 With guidance and support from adults and peers, focus on a topic and strengthen writing as needed by revising and editing.
CCSS.ELA-Literacy.W.2.6 With guidance and support from adults, use a variety of digital tools to produce and publish writing, including in collaboration with peers.
Research to Build and Present Knowledge
CCSS.ELA-Literacy.W.2.7 Participate in shared research and writing projects (e.g., read a number of books on a single topic to produce a report; record science observations).
CCSS.ELA-Literacy.W.2.8 Recall information from experiences or gather information from provided sources to answer a question.
(W.2.9 begins in grade 4)
Range of Writing
(W.2.10 begins in grade 3)

Third Grade
Text Types and Purposes
CCSS.ELA-Literacy.W.3.1 Write opinion pieces on topics or texts, supporting a point of view with reasons.
    CCSS.ELA-Literacy.W.3.1a Introduce the topic or text they are writing about, state an opinion, and create an organizational structure that lists reasons.
    CCSS.ELA-Literacy.W.3.1b Provide reasons that support the opinion.
    CCSS.ELA-Literacy.W.3.1c Use linking words and phrases (e.g., *because*, *therefore*, *since*, *for example*) to connect opinion and reasons.
    CCSS.ELA-Literacy.W.3.1d Provide a concluding statement or section.
CCSS.ELA-Literacy.W.3.2 Write informative/explanatory texts to examine a topic and convey ideas and information clearly.
    CCSS.ELA-Literacy.W.3.2a Introduce a topic and group related information together; include illustrations when useful to aiding comprehension.
    CCSS.ELA-Literacy.W.3.2b Develop the topic with facts, definitions, and details.
    CCSS.ELA-Literacy.W.3.2c Use linking words and phrases (e.g., *also*, *another*, *and*, *more*, *but*) to connect ideas within categories of information.
    CCSS.ELA-Literacy.W.3.2d Provide a concluding statement or section.
CCSS.ELA-Literacy.W.3.3 Write narratives to develop real or imagined experiences or events using effective technique, descriptive details, and clear event sequences.
    CCSS.ELA-Literacy.W.3.3a Establish a situation and introduce a narrator and/or characters; organize an event sequence that unfolds naturally.
    CCSS.ELA-Literacy.W.3.3b Use dialogue and descriptions of actions, thoughts, and feelings to develop experiences and events or show the response of characters to situations.
    CCSS.ELA-Literacy.W.3.3c Use temporal words and phrases to signal event order.
    CCSS.ELA-Literacy.W.3.3d Provide a sense of closure.
Production and Distribution of Writing
CCSS.ELA-Literacy.W.3.4 With guidance and support from adults, produce writing in which the development and organization are appropriate to task and purpose. (Grade-specific expectations for writing types are defined in standards 1–3 above.)
CCSS.ELA-Literacy.W.3.5 With guidance and support from peers and adults, develop and strengthen writing as needed by planning, revising, and editing. (Editing for conventions should demonstrate command of Language

standards 1-3 up to and including grade 3 here.)
CCSS.ELA-Literacy.W.3.6 With guidance and support from adults, use technology to produce and publish writing (using keyboarding skills) as well as to interact and collaborate with others.
Research to Build and Present Knowledge
CCSS.ELA-Literacy.W.3.7 Conduct short research projects that build knowledge about a topic.
CCSS.ELA-Literacy.W.3.8 Recall information from experiences or gather information from print and digital sources; take brief notes on sources and sort evidence into provided categories.
(W.3.9 begins in grade 4)
Range of Writing
CCSS.ELA-Literacy.W.3.10 Write routinely over extended time frames (time for research, reflection, and revision) and shorter time frames (a single sitting or a day or two) for a range of discipline-specific tasks, purposes, and audiences.

Fourth Grade
Text Types and Purposes
CCSS.ELA-Literacy.W.4.1 Write opinion pieces on topics or texts, supporting a point of view with reasons and information.
> CCSS.ELA-Literacy.W.4.1a Introduce a topic or text clearly, state an opinion, and create an organizational structure in which related ideas are grouped to support the writer's purpose.
> CCSS.ELA-Literacy.W.4.1b Provide reasons that are supported by facts and details.
> CCSS.ELA-Literacy.W.4.1c Link opinion and reasons using words and phrases (e.g., *for instance, in order to, in addition*).
> CCSS.ELA-Literacy.W.4.1d Provide a concluding statement or section related to the opinion presented.

CCSS.ELA-Literacy.W.4.2 Write informative/explanatory texts to examine a topic and convey ideas and information clearly.
> CCSS.ELA-Literacy.W.4.2a Introduce a topic clearly and group related information in paragraphs and sections; include formatting (e.g., headings), illustrations, and multimedia when useful to aiding comprehension.
> CCSS.ELA-Literacy.W.4.2b Develop the topic with facts, definitions, concrete details, quotations, or other information and examples related to the topic.
> CCSS.ELA-Literacy.W.4.2c Link ideas within categories of information using words and phrases (e.g., *another, for example, also, because*).
> CCSS.ELA-Literacy.W.4.2d Use precise language and domain-specific vocabulary to inform about or explain the topic.
> CCSS.ELA-Literacy.W.4.2e Provide a concluding statement or section related to the information or explanation presented.

CCSS.ELA-Literacy.W.4.3 Write narratives to develop real or imagined experiences or events using effective technique, descriptive details, and clear event sequences.
> CCSS.ELA-Literacy.W.4.3a Orient the reader by establishing a situation and introducing a narrator and/or characters; organize an event sequence that unfolds naturally.
> CCSS.ELA-Literacy.W.4.3b Use dialogue and description to develop experiences and events or show the responses of characters to situations.
> CCSS.ELA-Literacy.W.4.3c Use a variety of transitional words and phrases to manage the sequence of events.
> CCSS.ELA-Literacy.W.4.3d Use concrete words and phrases and sensory details to convey experiences and events precisely.
> CCSS.ELA-Literacy.W.4.3e Provide a conclusion that follows from the narrated experiences or events.

Production and Distribution of Writing
CCSS.ELA-Literacy.W.4.4 Produce clear and coherent writing in which the development and organization are appropriate to task, purpose, and audience. (Grade-specific expectations for writing types are defined in standards 1–3 above.)
CCSS.ELA-Literacy.W.4.5 With guidance and support from peers and adults, develop and strengthen writing as needed by planning, revising, and editing. (Editing for conventions should demonstrate command of Language standards 1-3 up to and including grade 4 here.)

CCSS.ELA-Literacy.W.4.6 With some guidance and support from adults, use technology, including the Internet, to produce and publish writing as well as to interact and collaborate with others; demonstrate sufficient command of keyboarding skills to type a minimum of one page in a single sitting.

Research to Build and Present Knowledge
CCSS.ELA-Literacy.W.4.7 Conduct short research projects that build knowledge through investigation of different aspects of a topic.
CCSS.ELA-Literacy.W.4.8 Recall relevant information from experiences or gather relevant information from print and digital sources; take notes and categorize information, and provide a list of sources.
CCSS.ELA-Literacy.W.4.9 Draw evidence from literary or informational texts to support analysis, reflection, and research.
> CCSS.ELA-Literacy.W.4.9a Apply *grade 4 Reading standards* to literature (e.g., "Describe in depth a character, setting, or event in a story or drama, drawing on specific details in the text [e.g., a character's thoughts, words, or actions].").
> CCSS.ELA-Literacy.W.4.9b Apply *grade 4 Reading standards* to informational texts (e.g., "Explain how an author uses reasons and evidence to support particular points in a text").

Range of Writing
CCSS.ELA-Literacy.W.4.10 Write routinely over extended time frames (time for research, reflection, and revision) and shorter time frames (a single sitting or a day or two) for a range of discipline-specific tasks, purposes, and audiences.

Fifth Grade
Text Types and Purposes
CCSS.ELA-Literacy.W.5.1 Write opinion pieces on topics or texts, supporting a point of view with reasons and information.
> CCSS.ELA-Literacy.W.5.1a Introduce a topic or text clearly, state an opinion, and create an organizational structure in which ideas are logically grouped to support the writer's purpose.
> CCSS.ELA-Literacy.W.5.1b Provide logically ordered reasons that are supported by facts and details.
> CCSS.ELA-Literacy.W.5.1c Link opinion and reasons using words, phrases, and clauses (e.g., *consequently*, *specifically*).
> CCSS.ELA-Literacy.W.5.1d Provide a concluding statement or section related to the opinion presented.

CCSS.ELA-Literacy.W.5.2 Write informative/explanatory texts to examine a topic and convey ideas and information clearly.
> CCSS.ELA-Literacy.W.5.2a Introduce a topic clearly, provide a general observation and focus, and group related information logically; include formatting (e.g., headings), illustrations, and multimedia when useful to aiding comprehension.
> CCSS.ELA-Literacy.W.5.2b Develop the topic with facts, definitions, concrete details, quotations, or other information and examples related to the topic.
> CCSS.ELA-Literacy.W.5.2c Link ideas within and across categories of information using words, phrases, and clauses (e.g., *in contrast*, *especially*).
> CCSS.ELA-Literacy.W.5.2d Use precise language and domain-specific vocabulary to inform about or explain the topic.
> CCSS.ELA-Literacy.W.5.2e Provide a concluding statement or section related to the information or explanation presented.

CCSS.ELA-Literacy.W.5.3 Write narratives to develop real or imagined experiences or events using effective technique, descriptive details, and clear event sequences.
> CCSS.ELA-Literacy.W.5.3a Orient the reader by establishing a situation and introducing a narrator and/or characters; organize an event sequence that unfolds naturally.
> CCSS.ELA-Literacy.W.5.3b Use narrative techniques, such as dialogue, description, and pacing, to develop experiences and events or show the responses of characters to situations.
> CCSS.ELA-Literacy.W.5.3c Use a variety of transitional words, phrases, and clauses to manage the sequence of events.
> CCSS.ELA-Literacy.W.5.3d Use concrete words and phrases and sensory details to convey experiences and events precisely.
> CCSS.ELA-Literacy.W.5.3e Provide a conclusion that follows from the narrated experiences or events.

Production and Distribution of Writing

CCSS.ELA-Literacy.W.5.4 Produce clear and coherent writing in which the development and organization are appropriate to task, purpose, and audience. (Grade-specific expectations for writing types are defined in standards 1–3 above.)

CCSS.ELA-Literacy.W.5.5 With guidance and support from peers and adults, develop and strengthen writing as needed by planning, revising, editing, rewriting, or trying a new approach. (Editing for conventions should demonstrate command of Language standards 1-3 up to and including grade 5 here.)

CCSS.ELA-Literacy.W.5.6 With some guidance and support from adults, use technology, including the Internet, to produce and publish writing as well as to interact and collaborate with others; demonstrate sufficient command of keyboarding skills to type a minimum of two pages in a single sitting.

Research to Build and Present Knowledge

CCSS.ELA-Literacy.W.5.7 Conduct short research projects that use several sources to build knowledge through investigation of different aspects of a topic.

CCSS.ELA-Literacy.W.5.8 Recall relevant information from experiences or gather relevant information from print and digital sources; summarize or paraphrase information in notes and finished work, and provide a list of sources.

CCSS.ELA-Literacy.W.5.9 Draw evidence from literary or informational texts to support analysis, reflection, and research.

> CCSS.ELA-Literacy.W.5.9a Apply *grade 5 Reading standards* to literature (e.g., "Compare and contrast two or more characters, settings, or events in a story or a drama, drawing on specific details in the text [e.g., how characters interact]").
>
> CCSS.ELA-Literacy.W.5.9b Apply *grade 5 Reading standards* to informational texts (e.g., "Explain how an author uses reasons and evidence to support particular points in a text, identifying which reasons and evidence support which point[s]").

Range of Writing

CCSS.ELA-Literacy.W.5.10 Write routinely over extended time frames (time for research, reflection, and revision) and shorter time frames (a single sitting or a day or two) for a range of discipline-specific tasks, purposes, and audiences.

Appendix D: Common Core State Standards for Speaking and Listening

Kindergarten
Comprehension and Collaboration
CCSS.ELA-Literacy.SL.K.1 Participate in collaborative conversations with diverse partners about *kindergarten topics and texts* with peers and adults in small and larger groups.
> CCSS.ELA-Literacy.SL.K.1a Follow agreed-upon rules for discussions (e.g., listening to others and taking turns speaking about the topics and texts under discussion).
> CCSS.ELA-Literacy.SL.K.1b Continue a conversation through multiple exchanges.

CCSS.ELA-Literacy.SL.K.2 Confirm understanding of a text read aloud or information presented orally or through other media by asking and answering questions about key details and requesting clarification if something is not understood.
CCSS.ELA-Literacy.SL.K.3 Ask and answer questions in order to seek help, get information, or clarify something that is not understood.
Presentation of Knowledge and Ideas
> CCSS.ELA-Literacy.SL.K.4 Describe familiar people, places, things, and events and, with prompting and support, provide additional detail.
> CCSS.ELA-Literacy.SL.K.5 Add drawings or other visual displays to descriptions as desired to provide additional detail.

CCSS.ELA-Literacy.SL.K.6 Speak audibly and express thoughts, feelings, and ideas clearly.

First Grade
Comprehension and Collaboration
CCSS.ELA-Literacy.SL.1.1 Participate in collaborative conversations with diverse partners about *grade 1 topics and texts* with peers and adults in small and larger groups.
> CCSS.ELA-Literacy.SL.1.1a Follow agreed-upon rules for discussions (e.g., listening to others with care, speaking one at a time about the topics and texts under discussion).
> CCSS.ELA-Literacy.SL.1.1b Build on others' talk in conversations by responding to the comments of others through multiple exchanges.
> CCSS.ELA-Literacy.SL.1.1c Ask questions to clear up any confusion about the topics and texts under discussion.

CCSS.ELA-Literacy.SL.1.2 Ask and answer questions about key details in a text read aloud or information presented orally or through other media.
CCSS.ELA-Literacy.SL.1.3 Ask and answer questions about what a speaker says in order to gather additional information or clarify something that is not understood.
Presentation **of Knowledge and Ideas**
> CCSS.ELA-Literacy.SL.1.4 Describe people, places, things, and events with relevant details, expressing ideas and feelings clearly.
> CCSS.ELA-Literacy.SL.1.5 Add drawings or other visual displays to descriptions when appropriate to clarify ideas, thoughts, and feelings.

CCSS.ELA-Literacy.SL.1.6 Produce complete sentences when appropriate to task and situation. (See grade 1 Language standards 1 and 3 for specific expectations.)

Second Grade
Comprehension and Collaboration
CCSS.ELA-Literacy.SL.2.1 Participate in collaborative conversations with diverse partners about *grade 2 topics and texts* with peers and adults in small and larger groups.
> CCSS.ELA-Literacy.SL.2.1a Follow agreed-upon rules for discussions (e.g., gaining the floor in respectful ways, listening to others with care, speaking one at a time about the topics and texts under discussion).
> CCSS.ELA-Literacy.SL.2.1b Build on others' talk in conversations by linking their comments to the remarks of others.
> CCSS.ELA-Literacy.SL.2.1c Ask for clarification and further explanation as needed about the topics and texts under discussion.

CCSS.ELA-Literacy.SL.2.2 Recount or describe key ideas or details from a text read aloud or information presented orally or through other media.
CCSS.ELA-Literacy.SL.2.3 Ask and answer questions about what a speaker says in order to clarify comprehension,

gather additional information, or deepen understanding of a topic or issue.
Presentation of Knowledge and Ideas
CCSS.ELA-Literacy.SL.2.4 Tell a story or recount an experience with appropriate facts and relevant, descriptive details, speaking audibly in coherent sentences.
CCSS.ELA-Literacy.SL.2.5 Create audio recordings of stories or poems; add drawings or other visual displays to stories or recounts of experiences when appropriate to clarify ideas, thoughts, and feelings.
CCSS.ELA-Literacy.SL.2.6 Produce complete sentences when appropriate to task and situation in order to provide requested detail or clarification. (See grade 2 Language standards 1 and 3 here for specific expectations.)

Third Grade
Comprehension and Collaboration
CCSS.ELA-Literacy.SL.3.1 Engage effectively in a range of collaborative discussions (one-on-one, in groups, and teacher-led) with diverse partners on *grade 3 topics and texts*, building on others' ideas and expressing their own clearly.
> CCSS.ELA-Literacy.SL.3.1a Come to discussions prepared, having read or studied required material; explicitly draw on that preparation and other information known about the topic to explore ideas under discussion.
> CCSS.ELA-Literacy.SL.3.1b Follow agreed-upon rules for discussions (e.g., gaining the floor in respectful ways, listening to others with care, speaking one at a time about the topics and texts under discussion).
> CCSS.ELA-Literacy.SL.3.1c Ask questions to check understanding of information presented, stay on topic, and link their comments to the remarks of others.
> CCSS.ELA-Literacy.SL.3.1d Explain their own ideas and understanding in light of the discussion.

CCSS.ELA-Literacy.SL.3.2 Determine the main ideas and supporting details of a text read aloud or information presented in diverse media and formats, including visually, quantitatively, and orally.
CCSS.ELA-Literacy.SL.3.3 Ask and answer questions about information from a speaker, offering appropriate elaboration and detail.
Presentation of Knowledge and Ideas
CCSS.ELA-Literacy.SL.3.4 Report on a topic or text, tell a story, or recount an experience with appropriate facts and relevant, descriptive details, speaking clearly at an understandable pace.
CCSS.ELA-Literacy.SL.3.5 Create engaging audio recordings of stories or poems that demonstrate fluid reading at an understandable pace; add visual displays when appropriate to emphasize or enhance certain facts or details.
CCSS.ELA-Literacy.SL.3.6 Speak in complete sentences when appropriate to task and situation in order to provide requested detail or clarification. (See grade 3 Language standards 1 and 3 here for specific expectations.)

Fourth Grade
Comprehension and Collaboration
CCSS.ELA-Literacy.SL.4.1 Engage effectively in a range of collaborative discussions (one-on-one, in groups, and teacher-led) with diverse partners on *grade 4 topics and texts*, building on others' ideas and expressing their own clearly.
> CCSS.ELA-Literacy.SL.4.1a Come to discussions prepared, having read or studied required material; explicitly draw on that preparation and other information known about the topic to explore ideas under discussion.
> CCSS.ELA-Literacy.SL.4.1b Follow agreed-upon rules for discussions and carry out assigned roles.
> CCSS.ELA-Literacy.SL.4.1c Pose and respond to specific questions to clarify or follow up on information, and make comments that contribute to the discussion and link to the remarks of others.
> CCSS.ELA-Literacy.SL.4.1d Review the key ideas expressed and explain their own ideas and understanding in light of the discussion.

CCSS.ELA-Literacy.SL.4.2 Paraphrase portions of a text read aloud or information presented in diverse media and formats, including visually, quantitatively, and orally.
CCSS.ELA-Literacy.SL.4.3 Identify the reasons and evidence a speaker provides to support particular points.
Presentation of Knowledge and Ideas
CCSS.ELA-Literacy.SL.4.4 Report on a topic or text, tell a story, or recount an experience in an organized manner, using appropriate facts and relevant, descriptive details to support main ideas or themes; speak clearly at an understandable pace.
CCSS.ELA-Literacy.SL.4.5 Add audio recordings and visual displays to presentations when appropriate to enhance the development of main ideas or themes.

CCSS.ELA-Literacy.SL.4.6 Differentiate between contexts that call for formal English (e.g., presenting ideas) and situations where informal discourse is appropriate (e.g., small-group discussion); use formal English when appropriate to task and situation. (See grade 4 Language standards 1 here for specific expectations.)

Fifth Grade
Comprehension and Collaboration
CCSS.ELA-Literacy.SL.5.1 Engage effectively in a range of collaborative discussions (one-on-one, in groups, and teacher-led) with diverse partners on *grade 5 topics and texts*, building on others' ideas and expressing their own clearly.
> CCSS.ELA-Literacy.SL.5.1a Come to discussions prepared, having read or studied required material; explicitly draw on that preparation and other information known about the topic to explore ideas under discussion.
> CCSS.ELA-Literacy.SL.5.1b Follow agreed-upon rules for discussions and carry out assigned roles.
> CCSS.ELA-Literacy.SL.5.1c Pose and respond to specific questions by making comments that contribute to the discussion and elaborate on the remarks of others.
> CCSS.ELA-Literacy.SL.5.1d Review the key ideas expressed and draw conclusions in light of information and knowledge gained from the discussions.

CCSS.ELA-Literacy.SL.5.2 Summarize a written text read aloud or information presented in diverse media and formats, including visually, quantitatively, and orally.
CCSS.ELA-Literacy.SL.5.3 Summarize the points a speaker makes and explain how each claim is supported by reasons and evidence.

Presentation of Knowledge and Ideas
CCSS.ELA-Literacy.SL.5.4 Report on a topic or text or present an opinion, sequencing ideas logically and using appropriate facts and relevant, descriptive details to support main ideas or themes; speak clearly at an understandable pace.
CCSS.ELA-Literacy.SL.5.5 Include multimedia components (e.g., graphics, sound) and visual displays in presentations when appropriate to enhance the development of main ideas or themes.
CCSS.ELA-Literacy.SL.5.6 Adapt speech to a variety of contexts and tasks, using formal English when appropriate to task and situation. (See grade 5 Language standards 1 and 3 here for specific expectations.)

Appendix E: Common Core State Standards for Language

Kindergarten
Conventions of Standard English
CCSS.ELA-Literacy.L.K.1 Demonstrate command of the conventions of standard English grammar and usage when writing or speaking.
> CCSS.ELA-Literacy.L.K.1a Print many upper- and lowercase letters.
> CCSS.ELA-Literacy.L.K.1b Use frequently occurring nouns and verbs.
> CCSS.ELA-Literacy.L.K.1c Form regular plural nouns orally by adding /s/ or /es/ (e.g., *dog, dogs; wish, wishes*).
> CCSS.ELA-Literacy.L.K.1d Understand and use question words (interrogatives) (e.g., *who, what, where, when, why, how*).
> CCSS.ELA-Literacy.L.K.1e Use the most frequently occurring prepositions (e.g., *to, from, in, out, on, off, for, of, by, with*).
> CCSS.ELA-Literacy.L.K.1f Produce and expand complete sentences in shared language activities.

CCSS.ELA-Literacy.L.K.2 Demonstrate command of the conventions of standard English capitalization, punctuation, and spelling when writing.
> CCSS.ELA-Literacy.L.K.2a Capitalize the first word in a sentence and the pronoun *I*
> CCSS.ELA-Literacy.L.K.2b Recognize and name end punctuation.
> CCSS.ELA-Literacy.L.K.2c Write a letter or letters for most consonant and short-vowel sounds (phonemes).
> CCSS.ELA-Literacy.L.K.2d Spell simple words phonetically, drawing on knowledge of sound-letter relationships.

Knowledge of Language
(L.K.3 begins in grade 2)

Vocabulary Acquisition and Use
CCSS.ELA-Literacy.L.K.4 Determine or clarify the meaning of unknown and multiple-meaning words and phrases based on kindergarten reading and content.
> CCSS.ELA-Literacy.L.K.4a Identify new meanings for familiar words and apply them accurately (e.g., knowing *duck* is a bird and learning the verb to *duck*).
> CCSS.ELA-Literacy.L.K.4b Use the most frequently occurring inflections and affixes (e.g., *-ed, -s, re-, un-, pre-, -ful, -less*) as a clue to the meaning of an unknown word.

CCSS.ELA-Literacy.L.K.5 With guidance and support from adults, explore word relationships and nuances in word meanings.
> CCSS.ELA-Literacy.L.K.5a Sort common objects into categories (e.g., shapes, foods) to gain a sense of the concepts the categories represent.
> CCSS.ELA-Literacy.L.K.5b Demonstrate understanding of frequently occurring verbs and adjectives by relating them to their opposites (antonyms).
> CCSS.ELA-Literacy.L.K.5c Identify real-life connections between words and their use (e.g., note places at school that are colorful).
> CCSS.ELA-Literacy.L.K.5d Distinguish shades of meaning among verbs describing the same general action (e.g., *walk, march, strut, prance*) by acting out the meanings.

CCSS.ELA-Literacy.L.K.6 Use words and phrases acquired through conversations, reading and being read to, and responding to texts.

First Grade
Conventions of Standard English
CCSS.ELA-Literacy.L.1.1 Demonstrate command of the conventions of standard English grammar and usage when writing or speaking.
> CCSS.ELA-Literacy.L.1.1a Print all upper- and lowercase letters.
> CCSS.ELA-Literacy.L.1.1b Use common, proper, and possessive nouns.
> CCSS.ELA-Literacy.L.1.1c Use singular and plural nouns with matching verbs in basic sentences (e.g., He hops; We hop).
> CCSS.ELA-Literacy.L.1.1d Use personal, possessive, and indefinite pronouns (e.g., I, me, my; they, them, their, anyone, everything).
> CCSS.ELA-Literacy.L.1.1e Use verbs to convey a sense of past, present, and future (e.g., Yesterday I

walked home; Today I walk home; Tomorrow I will walk home).
    CCSS.ELA-Literacy.L.1.1f Use frequently occurring adjectives.
    CCSS.ELA-Literacy.L.1.1g Use frequently occurring conjunctions (e.g., *and, but, or, so, because*).
    CCSS.ELA-Literacy.L.1.1h Use determiners (e.g., articles, demonstratives).
    CCSS.ELA-Literacy.L.1.1i Use frequently occurring prepositions (e.g., *during, beyond, toward*).
    CCSS.ELA-Literacy.L.1.1j Produce and expand complete simple and compound declarative, interrogative, imperative, and exclamatory sentences in response to prompts.
CCSS.ELA-Literacy.L.1.2 Demonstrate command of the conventions of standard English capitalization, punctuation, and spelling when writing.
    CCSS.ELA-Literacy.L.1.2a Capitalize dates and names of people.
    CCSS.ELA-Literacy.L.1.2b Use end punctuation for sentences.
    CCSS.ELA-Literacy.L.1.2c Use commas in dates and to separate single words in a series.
    CCSS.ELA-Literacy.L.1.2d Use conventional spelling for words with common spelling patterns and for frequently occurring irregular words.
    CCSS.ELA-Literacy.L.1.2e Spell untaught words phonetically, drawing on phonemic awareness and spelling conventions.

Knowledge of Language
(L.1.3 begins in grade 2)

Vocabulary Acquisition and Use
CCSS.ELA-Literacy.L.1.4 Determine or clarify the meaning of unknown and multiple-meaning words and phrases based on *grade 1 reading and content*, choosing flexibly from an array of strategies.
    CCSS.ELA-Literacy.L.1.4a Use sentence-level context as a clue to the meaning of a word or phrase.
    CCSS.ELA-Literacy.L.1.4b Use frequently occurring affixes as a clue to the meaning of a word.
    CCSS.ELA-Literacy.L.1.4c Identify frequently occurring root words (e.g., *look*) and their inflectional forms (e.g., *looks, looked, looking*).
CCSS.ELA-Literacy.L.1.5 With guidance and support from adults, demonstrate understanding of word relationships and nuances in word meanings.
    CCSS.ELA-Literacy.L.1.5a Sort words into categories (e.g., colors, clothing) to gain a sense of the concepts the categories represent.
    CCSS.ELA-Literacy.L.1.5b Define words by category and by one or more key attributes (e.g., a *duck* is a bird that swims; a *tiger* is a large cat with stripes).
    CCSS.ELA-Literacy.L.1.5c Identify real-life connections between words and their use (e.g., note places at home that are *cozy*).
    CCSS.ELA-Literacy.L.1.5d Distinguish shades of meaning among verbs differing in manner (e.g., *look, peek, glance, stare, glare, scowl*) and adjectives differing in intensity (e.g., large, gigantic) by defining or choosing them or by acting out the meanings.
CCSS.ELA-Literacy.L.1.6 Use words and phrases acquired through conversations, reading and being read to, and responding to texts, including using frequently occurring conjunctions to signal simple relationships (e.g., *because*).

Second Grade
Conventions of Standard English
CCSS.ELA-Literacy.L.2.1 Demonstrate command of the conventions of standard English grammar and usage when writing or speaking.
    CCSS.ELA-Literacy.L.2.1a Use collective nouns (e.g., *group*).
    CCSS.ELA-Literacy.L.2.1b Form and use frequently occurring irregular plural nouns (e.g., *feet, children, teeth, mice, fish*).
    CCSS.ELA-Literacy.L.2.1c Use reflexive pronouns (e.g., *myself, ourselves*).
    CCSS.ELA-Literacy.L.2.1d Form and use the past tense of frequently occurring irregular verbs (e.g., *sat, hid, told*).
    CCSS.ELA-Literacy.L.2.1e Use adjectives and adverbs, and choose between them depending on what is to be modified.
    CCSS.ELA-Literacy.L.2.1f Produce, expand, and rearrange complete simple and compound sentences (e.g., *The boy watched the movie; The little boy watched the movie; The action movie was watched by the little boy*).
CCSS.ELA-Literacy.L.2.2 Demonstrate command of the conventions of standard English capitalization, punctuation, and spelling when writing.

CCSS.ELA-Literacy.L.2.2a Capitalize holidays, product names, and geographic names.
CCSS.ELA-Literacy.L.2.2b Use commas in greetings and closings of letters.
CCSS.ELA-Literacy.L.2.2c Use an apostrophe to form contractions and frequently occurring possessives.
CCSS.ELA-Literacy.L.2.2d Generalize learned spelling patterns when writing words (e.g., *cage → badge; boy → boil*).
CCSS.ELA-Literacy.L.2.2e Consult reference materials, including beginning dictionaries, as needed to check and correct spellings.

Knowledge of Language
CCSS.ELA-Literacy.L.2.3 Use knowledge of language and its conventions when writing, speaking, reading, or listening.
CCSS.ELA-Literacy.L.2.3a Compare formal and informal uses of English

Vocabulary Acquisition and Use
CCSS.ELA-Literacy.L.2.4 Determine or clarify the meaning of unknown and multiple-meaning words and phrases based on grade 2 reading and content, choosing flexibly from an array of strategies.
CCSS.ELA-Literacy.L.2.4a Use sentence-level context as a clue to the meaning of a word or phrase.
CCSS.ELA-Literacy.L.2.4b Determine the meaning of the new word formed when a known prefix is added to a known word (e.g., *happy/unhappy, tell/retell*).
CCSS.ELA-Literacy.L.2.4c Use a known root word as a clue to the meaning of an unknown word with the same root (e.g., *addition, additional*).
CCSS.ELA-Literacy.L.2.4d Use knowledge of the meaning of individual words to predict the meaning of compound words (e.g., *birdhouse, lighthouse, housefly; bookshelf, notebook, bookmark*).
CCSS.ELA-Literacy.L.2.4e Use glossaries and beginning dictionaries, both print and digital, to determine or clarify the meaning of words and phrases.
CCSS.ELA-Literacy.L.2.5 Demonstrate understanding of word relationships and nuances in word meanings.
CCSS.ELA-Literacy.L.2.5a Identify real-life connections between words and their use (e.g., *describe foods that are spicy or juicy*).
CCSS.ELA-Literacy.L.2.5b Distinguish shades of meaning among closely related verbs (e.g., *toss, throw, hurl*) and closely related adjectives (e.g., *thin, slender, skinny, scrawny*).
CCSS.ELA-Literacy.L.2.6 Use words and phrases acquired through conversations, reading and being read to, and responding to texts, including using adjectives and adverbs to describe (e.g., *When other kids are happy that makes me happy*).

Third Grade
Conventions of Standard English
CCSS.ELA-Literacy.L.3 Demonstrate command of the conventions of standard English grammar and usage when writing or speaking.
CCSS.ELA-Literacy.L.3.1a Explain the function of nouns, pronouns, verbs, adjectives, and adverbs in general and their functions in particular sentences.
CCSS.ELA-Literacy.L.3.1b Form and use regular and irregular plural nouns.
CCSS.ELA-Literacy.L.3.1c Use abstract nouns (e.g., *childhood*).
CCSS.ELA-Literacy.L.3.1d Form and use regular and irregular verbs.
CCSS.ELA-Literacy.L.3.1e Form and use the simple (e.g., *I walked; I walk; I will walk*) verb tenses.
CCSS.ELA-Literacy.L.3.1f Ensure subject-verb and pronoun-antecedent agreement.*
CCSS.ELA-Literacy.L.3.1g Form and use comparative and superlative adjectives and adverbs, and choose between them depending on what is to be modified.
CCSS.ELA-Literacy.L.3.1h Use coordinating and subordinating conjunctions.
CCSS.ELA-Literacy.L.3.1i Produce simple, compound, and complex sentences.
CCSS.ELA-Literacy.L.3.2 Demonstrate command of the conventions of standard English capitalization, punctuation, and spelling when writing.
CCSS.ELA-Literacy.L.3.2a Capitalize appropriate words in titles.
CCSS.ELA-Literacy.L.3.2b Use commas in addresses.
CCSS.ELA-Literacy.L.3.2c Use commas and quotation marks in dialogue.
CCSS.ELA-Literacy.L.3.2d Form and use possessives.
CCSS.ELA-Literacy.L.3.2e Use conventional spelling for high-frequency and other studied words and for adding suffixes to base words (e.g., *sitting, smiled, cries, happiness*).

CCSS.ELA-Literacy.L.3.2f Use spelling patterns and generalizations (e.g., *word families, position-based spellings, syllable patterns, ending rules, meaningful word parts*) in writing words.

CCSS.ELA-Literacy.L.3.2g Consult reference materials, including beginning dictionaries, as needed to check and correct spellings.

Knowledge of Language

CCSS.ELA-Literacy.L.3.3 Use knowledge of language and its conventions when writing, speaking, reading, or listening.

CCSS.ELA-Literacy.L.3.3a Choose words and phrases for effect.*

CCSS.ELA-Literacy.L.3.3b Recognize and observe differences between the conventions of spoken and written standard English.

Vocabulary Acquisition and Use

CCSS.ELA-Literacy.L.3.4 Determine or clarify the meaning of unknown and multiple-meaning word and phrases based on grade 3 reading and content, choosing flexibly from a range of strategies.

CCSS.ELA-Literacy.L.3.4a Use sentence-level context as a clue to the meaning of a word or phrase.

CCSS.ELA-Literacy.L.3.4b Determine the meaning of the new word formed when a known affix is added to a known word (e.g., *agreeable/disagreeable, comfortable/uncomfortable, care/careless, heat/preheat*).

CCSS.ELA-Literacy.L.3.4c Use a known root word as a clue to the meaning of an unknown word with the same root (e.g., *company, companion*).

CCSS.ELA-Literacy.L.3.4d Use glossaries or beginning dictionaries, both print and digital, to determine or clarify the precise meaning of key words and phrases.

CCSS.ELA-Literacy.L.3.5 Demonstrate understanding of figurative language, word relationships and nuances in word meanings.

CCSS.ELA-Literacy.L.3.5a Distinguish the literal and nonliteral meanings of words and phrases in context (e.g., *take steps*).

CCSS.ELA-Literacy.L.3.5b Identify real-life connections between words and their use (e.g., describe people who are *friendly* or *helpful*).

CCSS.ELA-Literacy.L.3.5c Distinguish shades of meaning among related words that describe states of mind or degrees of certainty (e.g., *knew, believed, suspected, heard, wondered*).

CCSS.ELA-Literacy.L.3.6 Acquire and use accurately grade-appropriate conversational, general academic, and domain-specific words and phrases, including those that signal spatial and temporal relationships (e.g., *After dinner that night we went looking for them*).

Fourth Grade

Conventions of Standard English

CCSS.ELA-Literacy.L.4.1 Demonstrate command of the conventions of standard English grammar and usage when writing or speaking.

CCSS.ELA-Literacy.L.4.1a Use relative pronouns (*who, whose, whom, which, that*) and relative adverbs (*where, when, why*).

CCSS.ELA-Literacy.L.4.1b Form and use the progressive (e.g., *I was walking; I am walking; I will be walking*) verb tenses.

CCSS.ELA-Literacy.L.4.1c Use modal auxiliaries (e.g., *can, may, must*) to convey various conditions.

CCSS.ELA-Literacy.L.4.1d Order adjectives within sentences according to conventional patterns (e.g., *a small red bag* rather than *a red small bag*).

CCSS.ELA-Literacy.L.4.1e Form and use prepositional phrases.

CCSS.ELA-Literacy.L.4.1f Produce complete sentences, recognizing and correcting inappropriate fragments and run-ons.*

CCSS.ELA-Literacy.L.4.1g Correctly use frequently confused words (e.g., *to, too, two; there, their*).*

CCSS.ELA-Literacy.L.4.2 Demonstrate command of the conventions of standard English capitalization, punctuation, and spelling when writing.

CCSS.ELA-Literacy.L.4.2a Use correct capitalization.

CCSS.ELA-Literacy.L.4.2b Use commas and quotation marks to mark direct speech and quotations from a text.

CCSS.ELA-Literacy.L.4.2c Use a comma before a coordinating conjunction in a compound sentence.

CCSS.ELA-Literacy.L.4.2d Spell grade-appropriate words correctly, consulting references as needed.

Knowledge of Language

CCSS.ELA-Literacy.L.4.3 Use knowledge of language and its conventions when writing, speaking, reading, or listening.
> CCSS.ELA-Literacy.L.4.3a Choose words and phrases to convey ideas precisely.*
> CCSS.ELA-Literacy.L.4.3b Choose punctuation for effect.*
> CCSS.ELA-Literacy.L.4.3c Differentiate between contexts that call for formal English (e.g., presenting ideas) and situations where informal discourse is appropriate (e.g., small-group discussion).

Vocabulary Acquisition and Use

CCSS.ELA-Literacy.L.4.4 Determine or clarify the meaning of unknown and multiple-meaning words and phrases based on grade 4 reading and content, choosing flexibly from a range of strategies.
> CCSS.ELA-Literacy.L.4.4a Use context (e.g., definitions, examples, or restatements in text) as a clue to the meaning of a word or phrase.
> CCSS.ELA-Literacy.L.4.4b Use common, grade-appropriate Greek and Latin affixes and roots as clues to the meaning of a word (e.g., *telegraph, photograph, autograph*).
> CCSS.ELA-Literacy.L.4.4c Consult reference materials (e.g., dictionaries, glossaries, thesauruses), both print and digital, to find the pronunciation and determine or clarify the precise meaning of key words and phrases.

CCSS.ELA-Literacy.L.4.5 Demonstrate understanding of figurative language, word relationships, and nuances in word meanings.
> CCSS.ELA-Literacy.L.4.5a Explain the meaning of simple similes and metaphors (e.g., *as pretty as a picture*) in context.
> CCSS.ELA-Literacy.L.4.5b Recognize and explain the meaning of common idioms, adages, and proverbs.
> CCSS.ELA-Literacy.L.4.5c Demonstrate understanding of words by relating them to their opposites (antonyms) and to words with similar but not identical meanings (synonyms).

CCSS.ELA-Literacy.L.4.6 Acquire and use accurately grade-appropriate general academic and domain-specific words and phrases, including those that signal precise actions, emotions, or states of being (e.g., quizzed, whined, stammered) and that are basic to a particular topic (e.g., *wildlife, conservation,* and *endangered* when discussing animal preservation).

Fifth Grade

Conventions of Standard English

CCSS.ELA-Literacy.L.5.1 Demonstrate command of the conventions of standard English grammar and usage when writing or speaking.
> CCSS.ELA-Literacy.L.5.1a Explain the function of conjunctions, prepositions, and interjections in general and their function in particular sentences.
> CCSS.ELA-Literacy.L.5.1b Form and use the perfect (e.g., *I had walked; I have walked; I will have walked*) verb tenses.
> CCSS.ELA-Literacy.L.5.1c Use verb tense to convey various times, sequences, states, and conditions.
> CCSS.ELA-Literacy.L.5.1d Recognize and correct inappropriate shifts in verb tense.*
> CCSS.ELA-Literacy.L.5.1e Use correlative conjunctions (e.g., *either/or, neither/nor*).

CCSS.ELA-Literacy.L.5.2 Demonstrate command of the conventions of standard English capitalization, punctuation, and spelling when writing.
> CCSS.ELA-Literacy.L.5.2a Use punctuation to separate items in a series.*
> CCSS.ELA-Literacy.L.5.2b Use a comma to separate an introductory element from the rest of the sentence.
> CCSS.ELA-Literacy.L.5.2c Use a comma to set off the words *yes* and *no* (e.g., *Yes, thank you*), to set off a tag question from the rest of the sentence (e.g., *It's true, isn't it?*), and to indicate direct address (e.g., *Is that you, Steve?*).
> CCSS.ELA-Literacy.L.5.2d Use underlining, quotation marks, or italics to indicate titles of works.
> CCSS.ELA-Literacy.L.5.2e Spell grade-appropriate words correctly, consulting references as needed.

Knowledge of Language

CCSS.ELA-Literacy.L.5.3 Use knowledge of language and its conventions when writing, speaking, reading, or listening.
> CCSS.ELA-Literacy.L.5.3a Expand, combine, and reduce sentences for meaning, reader/listener interest, and style.
> CCSS.ELA-Literacy.L.5.3b Compare and contrast the varieties of English (e.g., *dialects, registers*) used

in stories, dramas, or poems.

Vocabulary Acquisition and Use

CCSS.ELA-Literacy.L.5.4 Determine or clarify the meaning of unknown and multiple-meaning words and phrases based on grade 5 reading and content, choosing flexibly from a range of strategies.

> CCSS.ELA-Literacy.L.5.4a Use context (e.g., cause/effect relationships and comparisons in text) as a clue to the meaning of a word or phrase.
>
> CCSS.ELA-Literacy.L.5.4b Use common, grade-appropriate Greek and Latin affixes and roots as clues to the meaning of a word (e.g., *photograph, photosynthesis*).
>
> CCSS.ELA-Literacy.L.5.4c Consult reference materials (e.g., dictionaries, glossaries, thesauruses), both print and digital, to find the pronunciation and determine or clarify the precise meaning of key words and phrases.

CCSS.ELA-Literacy.L.5.5 Demonstrate understanding of figurative language, word relationships, and nuances in word meanings.

> CCSS.ELA-Literacy.L.5.5a Interpret figurative language, including similes and metaphors, in context.
>
> CCSS.ELA-Literacy.L.5.5b Recognize and explain the meaning of common idioms, adages, and proverbs.
>
> CCSS.ELA-Literacy.L.5.5c Use the relationship between particular words (e.g., synonyms, antonyms, homographs) to better understand each of the words.

CCSS.ELA-Literacy.L.5.6 Acquire and use accurately grade-appropriate general academic and domain-specific words and phrases, including those that signal contrast, addition, and other logical relationships (e.g., *however, although, nevertheless, similarly, moreover, in addition*).

www.ingramcontent.com/pod-product-compliance
Lightning Source LLC
Chambersburg PA
CBHW080405170426
43193CB00016B/2815